CM

Cramer

Illustration used on early printings of a number of Stephen Foster's songs published by C. Holt Jr., New York, and Oliver Ditson, Boston.

Stephen Foster Song Book

Original Sheet Music of 40 Songs by
STEPHEN COLLINS FOSTER

Selected, with Introduction and Notes, by
RICHARD JACKSON
Head, Americana Collection, Library and Museum of Performing Arts,
New York Public Library

DOVER PUBLICATIONS, INC., NEW YORK

Published in Canada by General Publishing Company, Ltd.,
30 Lesmill Road, Don Mills, Toronto, Ontario.
Published in the United Kingdom by Constable and
Company, Ltd., 10 Orange Street, London WC 2.

Stephen Foster Song Book is a new work, first published by
Dover Publications, Inc., in 1974.

International Standard Book Numbers

Paperbound edition: 0-486-23048-1

Clothbound edition: 0-486-23086-4

Library of Congress Catalog Card Number: 73-93542

Manufactured in the United States of America
Dover Publications, Inc.
180 Varick Street
New York, N. Y. 10014

Introduction

Stephen Collins Foster was born on July 4, 1826 in Lawrenceville (a village founded by his father, William Barclay Foster) which subsequently became a suburb of Pittsburgh, Pennsylvania. While there exists a considerable amount of information on Foster's family history, there is no great wealth of factual data concerning Foster himself. Any narrative of his brief life and musical career is necessarily marked with gaps, question marks, and speculation.

We know that he spent his early life largely in and around Pittsburgh, that his formal academic and musical training was sparse, and that his family considered him a "problem child." We know that he began to compose at an early age and that he worked briefly as a clerk in offices in Pittsburgh and in Cincinnati from about 1846 to 1850. He married Jane McDowell in June 1850 and by this time had committed himself to a career as a songwriter, having published well over a dozen pieces, including the already famous "Oh! Susanna." He had also signed a contract for his work with the important New York music publisher Firth, Pond & Co.

We know that in 1852 he made his only visit to the South, a month's steamboat trip with his wife and a group of friends down the Ohio and Mississippi to New Orleans (he was in the city itself no longer than about two days). We do not know much about the character of his married life except that his wife and child (a daughter, Marion, born in 1851) were often separated from him. Was this because he was simply unable to support them or because of other deeper personal problems or, perhaps, a combination of these reasons? No one knows for sure. There were financial problems during the fourteen years of Foster's professional career, but they were not due to a lack of adequate compensation for his work. Popular myth still persists that he was continually victimized by publishers and promoters and suffered poverty while others got unjustly rich. This was not the case. Existing contracts and other documents show that Foster's royalties over the years constituted a modest but comfortable income by the standards of the time.

The difficulties were apparently caused by Foster's inability to manage his money wisely.

We know that during the 1850's he made trips to New York and lived there for brief periods, occasionally joined by his family. He had become famous by this time. His songs were immensely popular in this country and abroad. In 1860 he moved to New York permanently and apparently lived mostly alone in hotels until his death four years later. He became ill early in 1864 and on January 10 he fell in a faint in his room and cut a gash in his throat. He was taken to Bellevue Hospital and died there on January 13. Two of his brothers and his wife accompanied the body to Pittsburgh and he was buried on January 21 in Allegheny Cemetery.

Surrounding the documented facts about the life of Stephen Foster is a sea of legends and apocryphal stories. After his death, articles about him began to appear in newspapers and periodicals in different parts of the country, and they continued to appear for years. It seems as if practically everyone who had known him at one time or another, or who had met him once or twice, eventually got into print with his or her "true" story (no matter how dimly remembered) about the late songwriter. And it is probably this body of journalism that was largely responsible for establishing the Foster mythology. On the one hand he was practically worshipped as an artist of saintly qualities—loving, kind, gentle, fond of children and animals, devoted to his mother: the Saint Francis of Pittsburgh. On the other hand, he was said to be irresponsible, confused, a plagiarist and a hack, and—above all—a drunk. This last subject has generated a good deal of rich Victorian melodrama which has successfully obscured the facts, whatever they are. It should be remembered, however, that the accounts of Foster's enslavement by Demon Rum were given largely by respectable ladies and gentlemen at a time when the currents of the temperance movement were very strong.

The Foster legends are painted in primary colors. A truer image is perhaps something in pastels. And the most valuable clue to this is the voice that sounds so clearly in his songs.

Modern writers have begun to treat Foster with a seriousness that would have been quite beyond those earlier writers in their more-or-less homespun accounts. (This is not to suggest that all who wrote about Foster in the nineteenth century were amateurs. At least two prominent musical authors gave some coverage to Foster in their histories of American music: Frédéric Ritter in his *Music in America* (1883) and W. S. B. Matthews in his *A Hundred Years of Music in America* (1889). He received sympathetic treatment from both men, but their accounts are sketchy and superficial.) While certain writers have turned a strong new light on Foster, their interpretations are divergent. We are presented with certain contradictions, as in the antique mythology. The controversial area now is not so much the character of the man himself (though this is still debated) as it is his role in American culture and the nature of his tragedy.

In *America's Music* (2nd ed., 1966), the historian Gilbert Chase presents an excellent summary of Foster's life and works. The chief aim of Chase's book as a whole is to establish the supreme importance of popular and folk-rooted traditions in locating and assessing what is most vital and characteristic in the musical heritage of this country. Not surprisingly, then, he sees Foster's strength deriving from "the vitality of the frontier and a certain element of primitive simplicity" in conflict with "the genteel tradition of the urban fringe, dominated by sentimentality, conventionalism, and propriety." Foster's move into the popular theater, his decision to write for the "vulgar" minstrel stage, is judged by Chase to be his "first and greatest spiritual victory: to overcome the fear of not appearing respectable." Foster's tragedy is seen as his eventual capitulation to the forces of respectability, his "succumbing to drink and the genteel tradition." (Here Chase rings a slight variation on the Foster-as-deadbeat-drunk theme.)

An opposing view of Foster's significant move from the parlor to the stage is taken by Wilfrid Mellers, the British author-composer who produced in 1965 a personal critique of American music entitled *Music in a New Found Land*. While Mellers agrees that Foster was a victim of the oppressive gentility of his day, he feels that "his degeneration started . . . when he ceased to be an amateur songwriter and entered the commercial music racket," when "other men began to reap material profit from his world-wide popularity." In other words, Foster's move to the stage is interpreted as the beginning of his downfall rather than his salvation. Mellers sees Foster as a classic embodiment of the American loss of innocence, of the American nostalgia for a simple comfortable past. He believes that the songs "were not innocent as real folk music is innocent, for they expressed modern man's *consciousness* of loss."

The foregoing is a brief summary of some of the known facts about Stephen Foster, of the mythology that surrounds him, and a sample of modern critical opinion. But the chief concern of this collection (and the Notes at the end of the volume) is of course the Foster songs. Here is a cross-section of his work as a songwriter, including not only the most famous pieces but others that are representative of various aspects of his career. The chief value of the collection is that it presents the Foster songs plain—as he wrote them and as they were published during and just after his lifetime. Each song is given in a facsimile reproduction of a first or early edition.

The composer Virgil Thomson has written that Stephen Foster's music "is part of every American's culture who has any musical culture." If this statement is true (and it undoubtedly is), it is equally true that most Americans know the Foster songs only from arrangements and transcriptions. Furthermore, the average person "who has any musical culture" is probably not even aware of this situation. Those professionals who are aware—singers, conductors, record producers, editors and publishers—have quite deliberately turned away from the original versions. Foster apparently is not trusted: he must be somehow dressed up, modernized, "improved." Recourse to the originals should inevitably change this line of thinking. For here are the texts and melodies as originally conceived: so fresh and occasionally slightly different from familiar corrupt versions. Here are the accompaniments: carefully contrived, artful, simple—though not simple-minded. Here are dynamic markings and tempo indications supplied by the composer to guide interpretation.

As Foster emerges from the mists of folklore and is taken more seriously as a composer, the widespread bastardization of his songs will surely diminish. A collection such as the present one can only contribute to this end.

RICHARD JACKSON

New York City
February, 1974

Contents

The songs are arranged in alphabetical order (not counting "The" at the beginning of a title). The publisher given is the publisher of the sheet reprinted here; the date is that of the original publication. All the songs are reproduced from original early sheets, except the following, which are reproduced from facsimiles of the first editions: Nos. 1, 3, 9, 10, 17, 20, 26, 27, 32, 37, 38. The following songs are reproduced from original copies of the first editions: Nos. 2, 7, 11, 12, 14, 15, 16, 18, 19, 22, 23, 24, 25, 33, 34, 35, 36, 39. For "Gwine to Run All Night" (also known as "De Camptown Races"), see "Camptown Races." For "Way Down Upon de Swanee Ribber," see "Old Folks at Home." A chronological list of the songs follows this main listing.

Chronological List of Songs
by Year of Publication

1844: Open Thy Lattice Love

1846: There's a Good Time Coming

1848: Oh! Susanna
Old Uncle Ned

1849: Nelly Was a Lady

1850: Ah! May the Red Rose Live Alway!
Camptown Races
Nelly Bly
Way Down in Ca-i-ro

1851: Old Folks at Home
Ring de Banjo
Wilt Thou Be Gone, Love?

1852: Maggie By My Side
Massa's in de Cold Ground

1853: My Old Kentucky Home, Good Night
Old Dog Tray

1854: Jeanie with the Light Brown Hair

1855: Come Where My Love Lies Dreaming
Hard Times Comes Again No More
Some Folks
The Village Maiden

1856: Gentle Annie

1859: Thou Art the Queen of My Song

1860: Down Among the Cane-Brakes
The Glendy Burk
Old Black Joe

1861: Don't Bet our Money on de Shanghai

1862: Better Times Are Coming
Gentle Lena Clare
That's What's the Matter
There Are Plenty of Fish in the Sea
We Are Coming, Father Abraam, 300,000
More

1863: My Wife Is a Most Knowing Woman
Nothing But a Plain Old Soldier
The Song of All Songs
When This Dreadful War Is Ended
Willie Has Gone to the War

1864: Beautiful Dreamer
If You've Only Got a Moustache

1865: The Voices That Are Gone

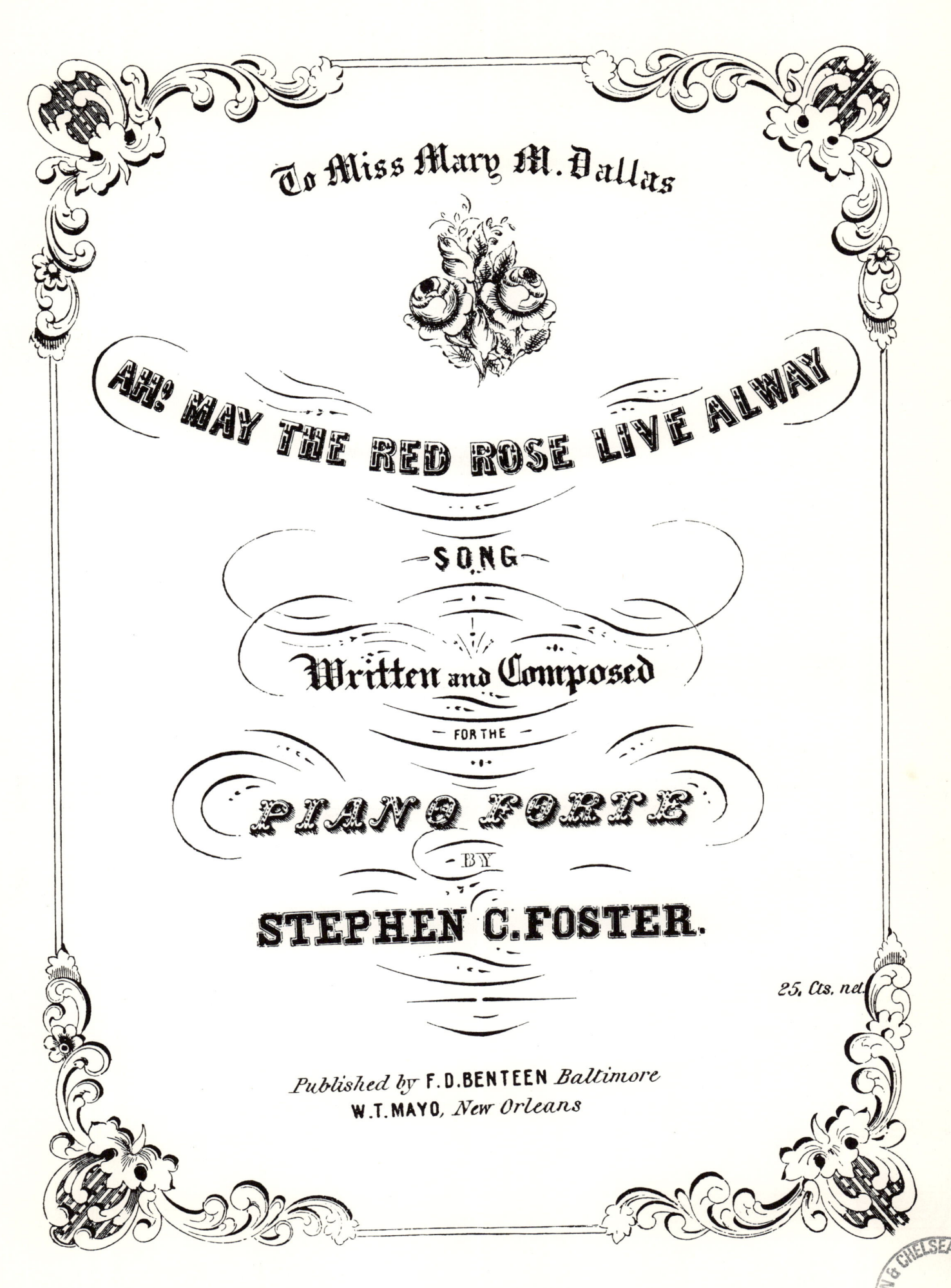

To Miss Mary M. Dallas

AH! MAY THE RED ROSE LIVE ALWAY

SONG

Written and Composed

FOR THE

PIANO FORTE

BY

STEPHEN C. FOSTER.

25. Cts. net.

Published by F. D. BENTEEN Baltimore
W. T. MAYO, New Orleans

"AH! MAY THE RED ROSE LIVE ALWAY!"

WORDS AND MUSIC BY   STEPHEN C. FOSTER.

Why should the beauti-ful e-ver weep? Why should the beau-ti--ful die!

Lending a charm to ev--'ry ray That falls on her cheeks of light,

Giving the zephyr kiss for kiss, And nur-sing the dew-drop bright—

Ah! may the red rose live al--way, To smile up-on earth and sky!

Why should the beauti-ful ever weep? Why should the beauti--ful die?

2.

Long may the daisies dance the field,
  Frolicking far and near!
Why should the innocent hide their heads?
  Why should the innocent fear?
Spreading their petals in mute delight
  When morn in its radiance breaks,
Keeping a floral festival
  Till the night-loving primrose wakes—
Long may the daisies dance the field,
  Frolicking far and near!
Why should the innocent hide their heads?
  Why should the innocent fear?

3.

Lulled be the dirge in the cypress bough,
  That tells of departed flowers!
Ah! that the butterfly's gilded wing
  Fluttered in evergreen bowers!
Sad is my heart for the blighted plants —
  Its pleasures are aye as brief —
They bloom at the young year's joyful call,
  And fade with the autumn leaf:
Ah! may the red rose live alway,
  To smile upon earth and sky!
Why should the beautiful ever weep!
  Why should the beautiful die!

Beautiful Dreamer.

"the last song ever written"

BY

STEPHEN C. FOSTER.

COMPOSED BUT A FEW DAYS PREVIOUS TO HIS DEATH.

— 3 —

NEW-YORK.

Published by Wm. A. Pond & Co. 547 Broadway.

Boston.
O. DITSON & Cº.

Milwaukee.
H. N. HEMPSTED.

Chicago.
ROOT & CADY.

Pittsburgh.
H. KLEBER & BRO.

Entered according to Act of Congress A.D 1864 by Wm. A. Pond &co. in the Clerks Office of the District Court of the Southern District of New-York.

BEAUTIFUL DREAMER.
SERENADE.

Words and Music
by
STEPHEN C. FOSTER.

Moderato.

Beau-ti-ful dream-er, wake un-to me,..... Star-light and dew-drops are wait-ing for thee;........................ Sounds of the rude world heard in the day,............. Lull'd by the moon-light have all pass'd a way!.................................

streamlet and sea;...... Then will all clouds of sor-row de-part,—

Beau-ti-ful dream-er, a-wake un-to me!............

Beau-ti-ful dream-er, a-wake un-to me!............

Ad Lib.

A Tempo.

Clayton.

FOSTER'S MELODIES

2½ EACH.

NEW-YORK:

Published by HORACE WATERS, No. 481 Broadway.

Boston: O. DITSON & Co., 277 Washington St.

Entered according to Act of Congress in the year 1862, by E. A. DAGGETT in the Clerks office of the Dist. Court for the Southern Dist. of New York.

Warren. Munc Stereotyper. 43 Centre.

BETTER TIMES ARE COMING.

WRITTEN AND COMPOSED BY STEPHEN C. FOSTER.

1. There are voi - ces of hope that are borne on the air, And our land will be freed from its clouds of des-pair, For brave men and true men to bat - tle have gone, And good times, good times are now com - ing on.

2

Abra'm Lincoln has the army and the navy in his hands,
While Seward keeps our honor bright abroad in foreign lands;
And Stanton is a man, who is sturdy as a rock,
With brave men to back him up and stand the battle's shock.   CHORUS.

3

Now McClellan is a leader and we'll let him take the sway,
For a man in his position, he should surely have his way.
Our nation's honor'd Scott, he has trusted to his might,
Your faith in McClellan put for we are sure he's right.   CHORUS.

4

Generals Lyon and Baker and Ellsworth now are gone,
But still we have some brave men to lead the soldiers on;
The noise of the battle will soon have died away,
And the darkness now upon us will be turn'd to happy day. CHORUS.

5

Generals Sigel and Halleck they have conquered in the West,
And Burnside, victorious, he rides the ocean's breast,
The traitors and the rebels will soon meet their doom;
Then peace and prosperity will dwell in every home.   CHORUS.

6

Captain Foote is commander of the Mississippi fleet,
For his flag he strikes and makes the traitors beat a quick retreat;
With iron-clad gun-boats he makes the rebels run,
While Grant makes our colors wave and glitter in the sun. CHORUS.

7

General Fremont the path-finder never lags behind,
He is gone to the mountains, new pathways to find,
His voice is for freedom, and his sword is for the right,
Then hail! noble Fremont the nation's delight.   CHORUS.

8

From the land of the Shamrock there's stuff that never yields,
For we've brave Colonel Corcoran, and gallant General Shields;
From Meagher soon we'll hear, for we know that he is true,
And stands for the honor of the Red, White and Blue.   CHORUS.

9

Here's health to Captain Ericsson, the Monitor and crew,
Who showed the southern chivalry a thing they never knew;
The Merrimac had slayed as St. Patrick did the toads,
Till Worden with the Monitor came into Hampton roads. CHORUS.

FOSTER'S
Plantation Melodies

AS SUNG BY THE

CHRISTY MINSTRELS,

Nº 1. OH LEMUEL.   Nº 2. DOLLY DAY.

„ 3. GWINE TO RUN ALL NIGHT.   4 . ANGELINA BAKER

Written, Composed & Arranged

BY

STEPHEN C. FOSTER.

25 Cts. Net.

Published by F. D. BENTEEN *Baltimore.*

W. T. MAYO *New Orleans.*

"GWINE TO RUN ALL NIGHT."

or

DE CAMPTOWN RACES.

Words and music by

S. C. Foster.

2

De long tail filly and de big black hoss___ Doo-dah! doo-dah!

Dey fly de track and dey both cut across___ Oh! doo-dah-day!

De blind hoss sticken in a big mud hole___ Doo-dah! doo-dah!

Can't touch bottom wid a ten foot pole___ Oh! doo-dah-day!

CHO: Gwine to run all night! &c.

3

Old muley cow come on to de track___ Doo-dah! doo-dah!

De bob-tail fling her ober his back___ Oh! doo-dah-day!

Den fly along like a rail-road car___ Doo-dah! doo-dah!

Runnin' a race wid a shootin' star___ Oh! doo-dah-day!

CHO: Gwine to run all night! &c.

4

See dem flyin' on a ten mile heat___ Doo-dah! doo-dah!

Round de race track, den repeat___ Oh! doo-dah-day!

I win my money on de bob-tail nag___ Doo-dah! doo-dah!

I keep my money in an old tow-bag___ Oh! doo-dah-day!

CHO: Gwine to run all nigh! &c.

Webb.

COME WHERE MY LOVE LIES DREAMING

Quartette

WRITTEN AND COMPOSED BY

STEPHEN C. FOSTER.

New York
PUBLISHED BY WM. A. POND & CO. 547 BROADWAY.

Cincinnati.
W. F. COLBURN.

St. Louis.
W. W. WAKELAM.

New Orleans.
P. P. WERLEIN.

Entered according to Act of Congress AD 1855 by Firth Pond & Co in the Clerks Office of the Dist Ct of the Southern District of N.Y.

COME WHERE MY LOVE LIES DREAMING.

QUARTETTE.

Written and Composed by **STEPHEN C. FOSTER.**

Soft is her slum_ber; Thoughts bright and free Dance through her dreams Like gushing mel_o_dy;

Soft is her slum_ber; Thoughts bright and free Dance through her dreams Like gushing mel_o_dy;

Light is her young heart, Light may it be: Come where my love lies dream _ _ ing.

Light is her young heart, Light may it be: Come where my love lies dream _ _ ing.

Dream _ _ _ ing the hap_py hours, Dreaming the hap_py hours a_way;

Come where my love lies dream_ing, Dream _ ing,

Come where my love lies dream_ing, Dreaming the hap_py hours a_way;

Grave par Lawson.

FOSTER'S MELODIES

Nº 52.

Don't bet your money on de Shanghai

PLANTATION SONG

WRITTEN AND COMPOSED BY

STEPHEN C. FOSTER.

Author of GLENDY BURK. OLD FOLKS AT HOME. &C.&C.&C.

3

NEW YORK.
Published by FIRTH.POND.&CO 547 Broadway

Boston.
O.DITSON & CO.

Cincinnati.
C.Y.FONDA.

New Orleans.
P. P. WERLEIN.

Pittsburgh.
H.KLEBER & BRO.

DON'T BET YOUR MONEY ON DE SHANGHAI.

WRITTEN AND COMPOSED BY STEPHEN C. FOSTER.

Moderato con spirito.

De Shang - hai chick - en, when you put him in de pit, He'll eat a loaf of bread up, but he can't fight a bit De Shang - hai fid - dle is a fun - ny lit - tle thing And eb - ry time you tune him up he goes ching ching.

Oh! de Shang-hai! Don't bet your mon-ey on de Shang-hai,

Take de lit-tle chick-en in de mid-dle ob de ring But

don't bet your money on de Shang-hai.

1.

De Shanghai chicken when you put him in de pit

He'll eat a loaf of bread up but he can't fight a bit

De Shanghai fiddle is a funny little thing

And ebry time you tune him up he goes ching! ching!

> *Chorus* — Oh! de Shanghai!
>
> Don't bet your money on de Shanghai!
>
> Take de little chicken in de middle of de ring
>
> But don't bet your money on de Shanghai.

2.

I go to de fair for to see de funny fowls

De double headed pigion and de one eyed owls

De old lame goose wid no web between his toes

He kills himself a laughing when de Shanghai crows.

> *Chorus* — Oh! de Shanghai! &c. —

3.

De Shanghai's tall but his appetite is small

He'll only swallow ebry thing that he can overhaul

Four bags of wheat just as certain as your born

A bushel of potatoes and a tub full of corn.

> *Chorus* — Oh! de Shanghai! &c. —

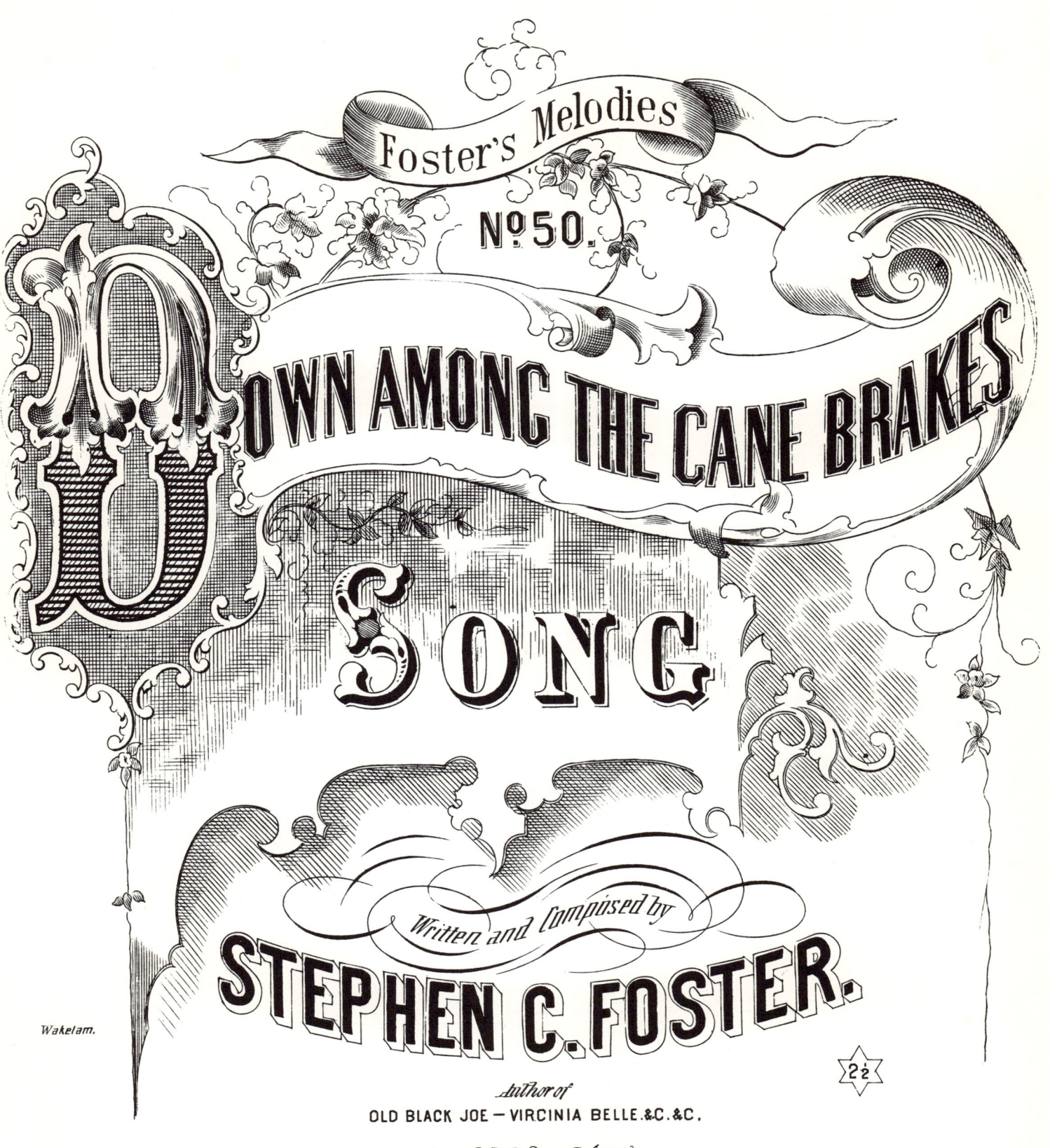

Foster's Melodies

Nº 50.

DOWN AMONG THE CANE BRAKES

SONG

Written and Composed by

STEPHEN C. FOSTER.

Wakelam.

Author of

OLD BLACK JOE — VIRGINIA BELLE. &C. &C.

NEW YORK
Published by FIRTH. POND & CO. 547 Broadway.

Boston.
O. DITSON & CO.

Cincinnati.
C. Y. FONDA.

Pittsburgh.
H. KLEBER & BRO

DOWN AMONG

THE CANE-BRAKES.

·Written and Composed by S.C.Foster.

3.VER: There lived my mo·ther dear (Gone from this world I fear)
4.VER: There lived a love·ly one, Who like the rest has gone,—
5.VER: Long years have gli·ded by Since then I breathed each sigh,—

There rang our voi·ces clear Down a·mong the cane-brakes.
She might have been my own Down a·mong the cane-brakes.
May I re··turn to die Down a·mong the cane-brakes.

GENTLE ANNIE.

WRITTEN AND COMPOSED BY S.C.FOSTER.

Andante mosso.

Thou wilt come no more, gen_tle An_nie, Like a

flower thy spi_rit did de_part; Thou art gone, a _ _ las! like the

many That have bloomed in the summer of my heart.

CHORUS.

Shall we ne_ver more be_hold thee; ne_ver hear thy winning voice a_

_gain _ When the Spring time comes, gen_tle Annie, When the

wild flowers are scattered o'er the plain?

SECOND VERSE.

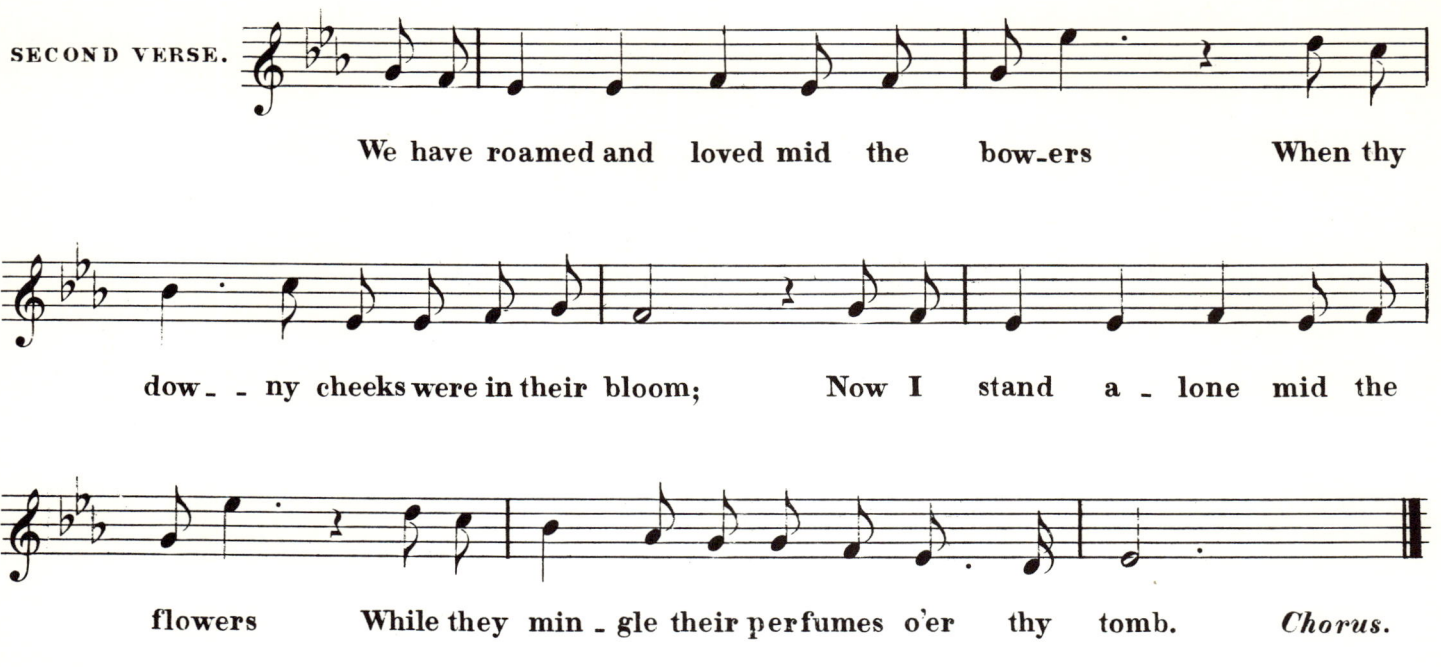

We have roamed and loved mid the bow-ers When thy dow_ _ ny cheeks were in their bloom; Now I stand a _ lone mid the flowers While they min _ gle their perfumes o'er thy tomb. *Chorus.*

THIRD VERSE.

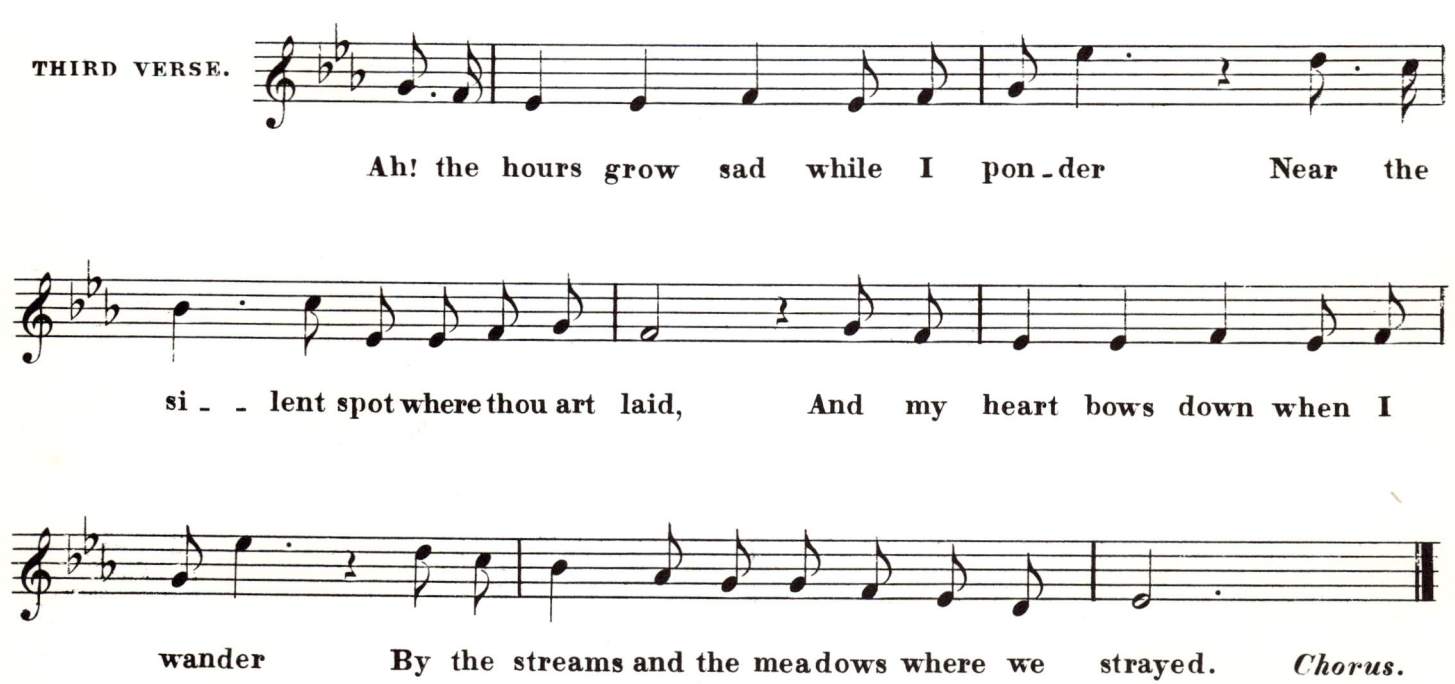

Ah! the hours grow sad while I pon_der Near the si_ _ lent spot where thou art laid, And my heart bows down when I wander By the streams and the meadows where we strayed. *Chorus.*

Gentle Lena Clare

Words & Music by

STEPHEN C. FOSTER.

NEW YORK
Published by S. T. GORDON 706 Broadway.

Boston.
HENRY TOLMAN & CO.

Philª
LEE & WALKER.

GENTLE LENA CLARE.

Written and Composed by
STEPHEN C. FOSTER.

I'm think- ing of sweet Le - na Clare, With
I love her care - less win - ning ways, I

deep blue eyes and wav - ing hair, Her voice is soft, her
love her wild and bird - like lays, I love the grass where-

face is   fair   My   gen - tle   Le - na   Clare.
on   she   strays   My   gen - tle   Le - na   Clare.

CHORUS.

Tenor.

Gen - tle   Le - na   Clare   My   dear lov'd Le - na   Clare   Her

Air.

Gen - tle   Le - na   Clare   My   dear lov'd Le - na   Clare   Her

Alto.

Gen - tle   Le - na   Clare   My   dear lov'd Le - na   Clare   Her

Bass.

3.

Her home is in the shady glen,

When summer comes I'll seek again,

On mountain height and lowland plain;

My gentle Lena Clare.

CHORUS. Gentle Lena Clare, &c.

NEW YORK
Published by FIRTH, POND & CO. 547 Broadway.

Boston.
O. DITSON & CO.

Cincinnati.
C. Y. FONDA.

Pittsburgh.
H. KLEBER & BRO

THE GLENDY BURK

WORDS AND MUSIC, BY STEPHEN C. FOSTER.

De Glen·dy Burk   is a mighty fast boat, Wid a mighty fast cap·tain   too;   He

sits up dah   on de hur·ri·cane roof And he keeps his eye   on de crew.   I

cant stay here, for dey work too hard; I'm bound to leave dis town; I'll

Ent'd according to Act of Congress A.D 1860 by Firth, Pond & Co in the Clerks Office of the Dis't Court for the South'n District of N.Y

42

FOSTER'S MELODIES

Nº 28

'Tis the Song the Sigh of the Weary.

HARD TIMES COME AGAIN NO MORE

MASSAS IN THE COLD GROUND.

FAREWELL MY LILLY DEAR.

MOLLY DO YOU LOVE ME.

LITTLE ELLA.

MY OLD KENTUCKY HOME GOODNIGHT.

STAY SUMMER BREATH.

NELLY WAS A LADY.

WILLIE WE HAVE MISSED YOU.

OH BOYS CARRY ME LONG.

OLD MEMORIES.

CAMPTOWN RACES.

WRITTEN AND COMPOSED

BY

STEPHEN COLLINS FOSTER

OLD DOG TRAY.

UNCLE NED.

NELLY BLY.

OLD FOLKS AT HOME.

ELLEN BAYNE.

JEANIE WITH THE LIGHT BROWN HAIR.

MAGGIE BY MY SIDE.

WILLIE MY BRAVE.

SUSANNA EULALIE.

COME AGAIN.

COME WITH THY SWEET VOICE.

PIANO

GUITAR

25 Cts. nett.

NEW YORK

PUBLISHED BY FIRTH, POND & Cº I FRANKLIN SQUARE

Pittsburgh
H. KLEBER.

Cincinnati
COLBURN & FIELD.

Louisville
FAULDS. STONE & MORSE.

St. Louis
W. W. WAKELAM.

New Orleans
P. P. WERLEIN.

HARD TIMES COME AGAIN NO MORE.

Poetry and Music by STEPHEN C. FOSTER.

While we seek mirth and beauty and mu_sic light and gay There are frail forms faint_ing at the

Let us pause in life's pleasures and count its many tears While we all sup sorrow with the

door: Though their voi ___ ces are si__lent, their plead_ing looks will say __ Oh!

poor: There's a song that will lin_ger for__ev__er in our ears; __ Oh!

Hard Times, come a__gain no more.

Hard Times, come a_gain no more.

Chorus.

'Tis the song, the sigh of the weary; __

Hard Times, Hard Times, come a_gain no more: Many days you have lingered a-round my cab_in door; Oh! Hard Times, come a_gain no more.

3

There's a pale drooping maiden who toils her life away
With a worn heart whose better days are o'er:
Though her voice would be merry, 'tis sighing all the day_
Oh! Hard Times, come again no more.
            Chorus.   Tis the song &c

4

'Tis a sigh that is wafted across the troubled wave,
'Tis a wail that is heard upon the shore,
'Tis a dirge that is murmured around the lowly grave,—
Oh! Hard Times, come again no more.
            Chorus.   Tis the song &c

Chorus arranged for four voices.

TENOR.

'Tis the song, the sigh of the wea_ry; Hard Times, Hard Times, come again no more; Many

I. SOPRANO.

'Tis the song, the sigh of the wea_ry; Hard Times, Hard Times, come again no more; Many

II. SOPRANO.

BASS.

days you have lingered around my cabin door, Oh! Hard Times, come again no more.

days you have lingered around my cabin door, Oh! Hard Times, come again no more.

8va

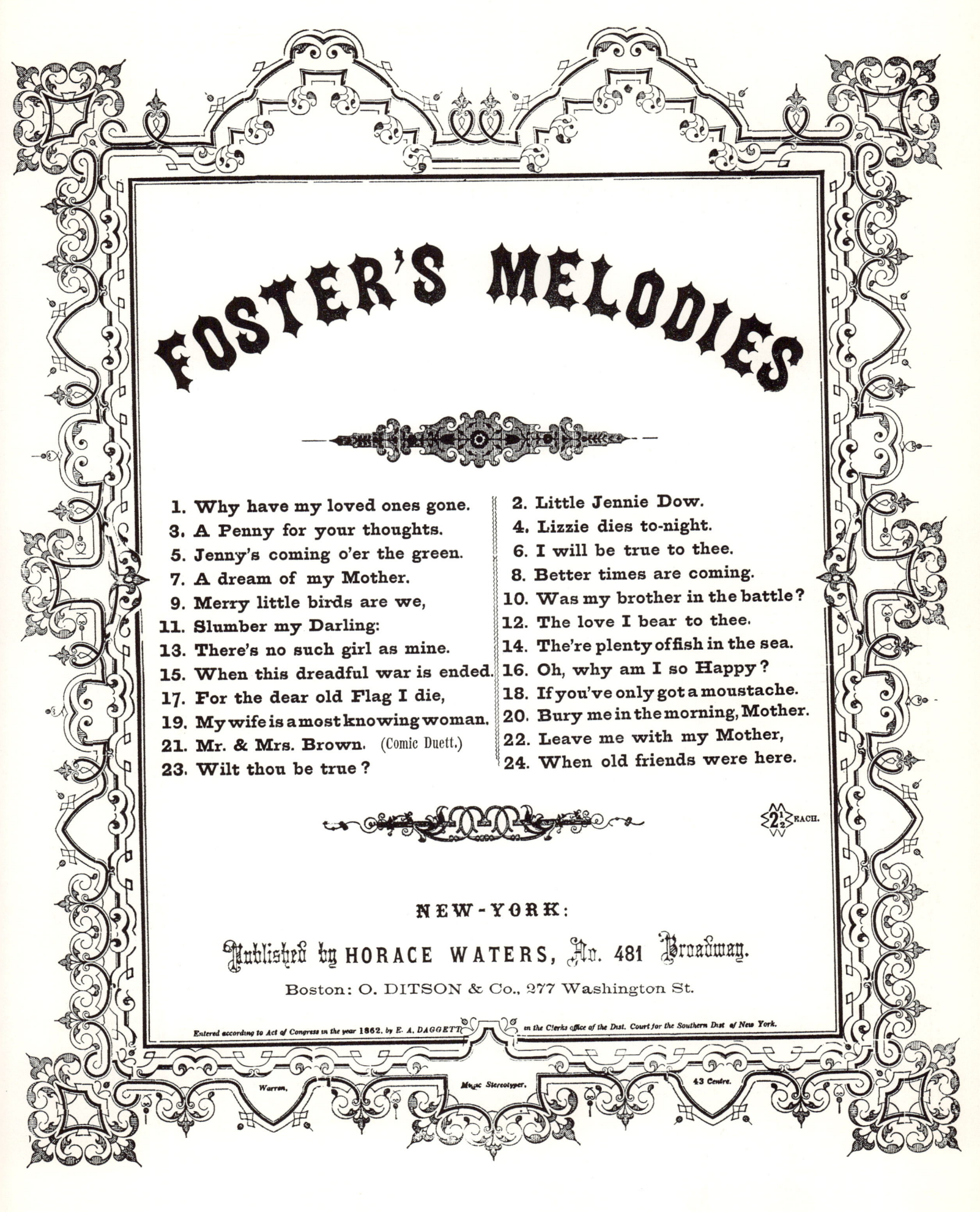

FOSTER'S MELODIES

1. Why have my loved ones gone.
2. Little Jennie Dow.
3. A Penny for your thoughts.
4. Lizzie dies to-night.
5. Jenny's coming o'er the green.
6. I will be true to thee.
7. A dream of my Mother.
8. Better times are coming.
9. Merry little birds are we,
10. Was my brother in the battle?
11. Slumber my Darling:
12. The love I bear to thee.
13. There's no such girl as mine.
14. The're plenty of fish in the sea.
15. When this dreadful war is ended.
16. Oh, why am I so Happy?
17. For the dear old Flag I die,
18. If you've only got a moustache.
19. My wife is a most knowing woman.
20. Bury me in the morning, Mother.
21. Mr. & Mrs. Brown. (Comic Duett.)
22. Leave me with my Mother,
23. Wilt thou be true?
24. When old friends were here.

2½ EACH.

NEW-YORK:

Published by HORACE WATERS, No. 481 Broadway.

Boston: O. DITSON & Co., 277 Washington St.

Entered according to Act of Congress in the year 1862, by E. A. DAGGETT in the Clerks office of the Dist. Court for the Southern Dist of New York.

Warren,   Music Stereotyper,   43 Centre.

IF YOU'VE ONLY GOT A MOUSTACHE.

(COMIC SONG.)

Written by GEORGE COOPER.

Composed by STEPHEN C. FOSTER.

1. Oh! all of you poor sin-gle men, Don't ev-er give up in des-pair, For there's al-ways a chance while there's

life   To cap - ture the hearts of the fair,   No

mat - ter what may be your age,   You al - ways may cut a fine

dash,   You will suit all the girls to a hair   If you've

on - - ly got a mous-tache,   A mous-tache,   a mous-

tache,   If   you've on - - - - ly   got   a   mous - tache.

2.

No matter for manners or style,
    No matter for birth or for fame,
All these *used* to have something to do
    With young ladies changing their name,
There's no reason now to despond,
    Or go and do any thing rash,
For you'll do though you can't raise a cent,
    If you'll only raise a moustache !
        A moustache, a moustache,
        If you'll only raise a moustache.

3.

Your head may be thick as a block,
    And empty as any foot-ball,
Oh ! your eyes may be green as the grass
    Your heart just as hard as a wall.
Yet take the advice that I give,
    You'll soon gain affection and cash,
And will be all the rage with the girls,
    If you'll only get a moustache,
        A moustache, a moustache,
        If you'll only get a moustache.

4.

I once was in sorrow and tears
    Because I was jilted you know,
So right down to the river I ran
    To quickly dispose of my woe,
A good friend he gave me advice
    And timely prevented the splash,
Now at home I've a wife and ten heirs,
    And all through a handsome moustache,
        A moustache, a moustache,
        And all through a handsome moustache.

JEANIE WITH THE LIGHT BROWN HAIR.

Poetry and Music ⸺ by Stephen C. Foster.

I dream of Jea _ nie with the light brown hair,

Borne, like a va _ _ _ por, on the sum _ mer air: I

see   her trip__ping where the bright   streams play,

Hap_py   as the dai___sies that dance   on her   way.

Ma__ny were the wild   notes her mer__ry voice would pour,

Ma__ny were the blithe   birds that war__bled them o'er: Oh!.......... I

ad lib:

dream   of   Jea_nie   with   the   light   brown   hair,

Float_ing,   like   a   va_por, on   the   soft   sum_mer   air.

Ral_ _len_ _ _tan_ _ _ _do.

8va ... *loco.*

tempo.

I   long   for   Jea_ _nie   with   the   day_ _ _dawn   smile,
I   sigh   for   Jea_ _nie,   but   her   light   form   strayed

To Miss Eliza T. Denniston.

MAGGIE BY MY SIDE.

SONG

WRITTEN & COMPOSED BY

STEPHEN C. FOSTER.

NEW YORK.
Published by FIRTH POND & Cº 1 Franklin Sq

Pittsburgh, H. KLEBER.

25¢ net

Cincinnati, DUNTON & THURSTON.

MAGGIE BY MY SIDE.

Poetry & Music by S. C. FOSTER.

The land of my home is flitting, Flitting from my view; A gale in the sails is sit_ting,

Toils the merry crew. Here let my home be, On the waters wide: I

MASSA'S IN DE COLD GROUND

As sung by

Christy's Minstrels

WRITTEN & COMPOSED BY

STEPHEN C. FOSTER.

Just published by the same Author
FAREWELL MY LILLY DEAR.

Greene Sc.

25 ¢ net.

NEW YORK.
Published by FIRTH POND & Cᵒ 1 Franklin Sq.

Baltimore. F.D.BENTEEN & Cᵒ   Pittsburgh.   H. KLEBER.

MASSA'S IN DE COLD GROUND.

Stephen C. Foster.

Poco Lento.

Round de meadows am a ring _ ing De dark _ eys' mourn _ _ ful song,

While de mocking-bird am sing _ _ ing, Hap_py as de day am long.

II.Ver:

When de au_tumn leaves were fall _ ing, When de days were cold, 'Twas

hard to hear old mas_sa call_ing, Cayse he was so weak and old.

Now de or _ ange tree am bloom_ing On de san _ _ dy shore,

Now de sum_mer days am com _ ing, Mas _ sa neb_ber calls no more. CHORUS.

III.Ver:

Mas _ _ sa made de dark_eys love him, Cayse he was so kind,

Now dey sad _ ly weep a _ bove him, Mourning cayse he leave dem be_hind. I

can _ _ not work be _ fore to _ mor_row, Cayse de tear drops flow, I

try to drive a _ way my sor _ _ row Pick_in on de old ban_jo. CHORUS.

MY OLD KENTUCKY HOME, GOOD NIGHT

FOSTER'S PLANTATION MELODIES

Nº 20

As Sung by

Christy's Minstrels

Nº 18. FAREWELL MY LILLY DEAR.
Nº 19. MASSA'S IN THE COLD GROUND.

Written and Composed by

STEPHEN C. FOSTER.

25ⁿᵉᵗ nett.

NEW YORK
Published by FIRTH, POND & CO. 1 Franklin Square,

Pittsburgh,
H. KLEBER.

Cleveland,
HOLBROOK & LONG.

Sᵗ Louis.
BALMER & WEBER.

MY OLD KENTUCKY HOME, GOOD-NIGHT!

Words and Music by

STEPHEN C. FOSTER.

POCO ADAGIO.

The sun shines bright in the old Kentucky home, 'Tis summer, the darkies are gay, The

corn top's ripe and the meadow's in the bloom While the birds make music all the day. The young folks roll on the lit_tle cabin floor, All merry, all happy and bright: By'n by Hard Times comes a knocking at the door, Then my old Kentucky Home, good night!

CHORUS

Weep no more, my lady, oh! weep no more to_day! We will sing one song For the old Kentucky Home, For the old Kentucky Home, far a_way.

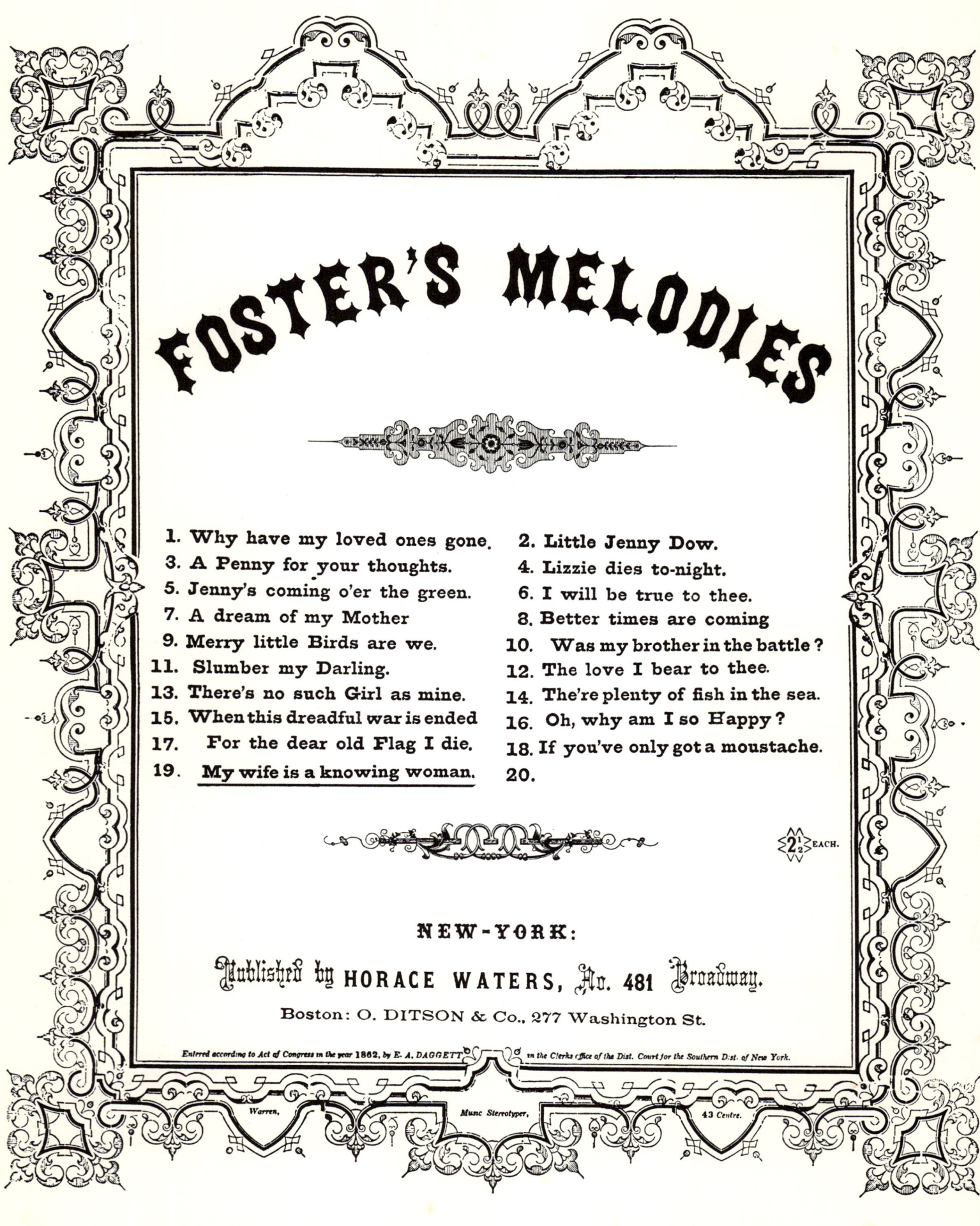

FOSTER'S MELODIES

2½ EACH.

NEW-YORK:

Published by HORACE WATERS, No. 481 Broadway.

Boston: O. DITSON & Co., 277 Washington St.

Warren,   Music Stereotyper,   43 Centre.

MY WIFE IS A MOST KNOWING WOMAN.

Poetry by GEORGE COOPER.

Music by STEPHEN C. FOSTER.

Vivace.

1. My wife is a most know - ing wo - man, She al - ways is find - ing me out, She

never will hear ex-plan-a-tions But in-stant-ly puts me to rout, There's no use to try to de-ceive her, If out with my friends, night or day, In the most in-con-ceiv-a-ble man-ner She tells where I've been right a-way, She

says that I'm "mean" and "in-hu-man" Oh! my wife is a most know-ing

wo-man.

2.

She would have been hung up for witchcraft
   If she had lived sooner, I know,
There's no hiding any thing from her,
   She knows what I do—where I go ;
And if I come in after midnight
   And say "I have been to the lodge,"
Oh, she says while she flies in a fury,
   "Now don't think to play such a dodge !
It's all very fine, but wont do, man,"
   Oh, my wife is a most knowing woman.

3.

Not often I go out to dinner
   And come home a little "so so,"
I try to creep up through the hall-way,
   As still as a mouse, on tip-toe,
She's sure to be waiting up for me
   And then comes a nice little scene,
"What, you tell me you're sober, you wretch you,
   Now don't think that I am so green !
My life is quite worn out with you, man,"
   Oh, my wife is a most knowing woman !

4.

She knows *me* much better than *I do*,
   Her eyes are like those of a lynx,
Though how she discovers my secrets
   Is a riddle would puzzle a sphynx,
On fair days, when we go out walking,
   If ladies look at me askance,
In the most harmless way, I assure you,
   My wife gives me, oh ! such a glance,
And says "all these insults you'll rue, man,"
   Oh, my wife is a most knowing woman.

5.

Yes, I must give all of my friends up
   If I would live happy and quiet ;
One might as well be 'neath a tombstone
   As live in confusion and riot.
'This life we all know is a short one,
   While *some* tongues are long, heaven knows,
And a miserable life is a husbands,
   Who numbers his wife with his foes,
I'll stay at home now like a true man,
   For my wife is a most knowing woman.

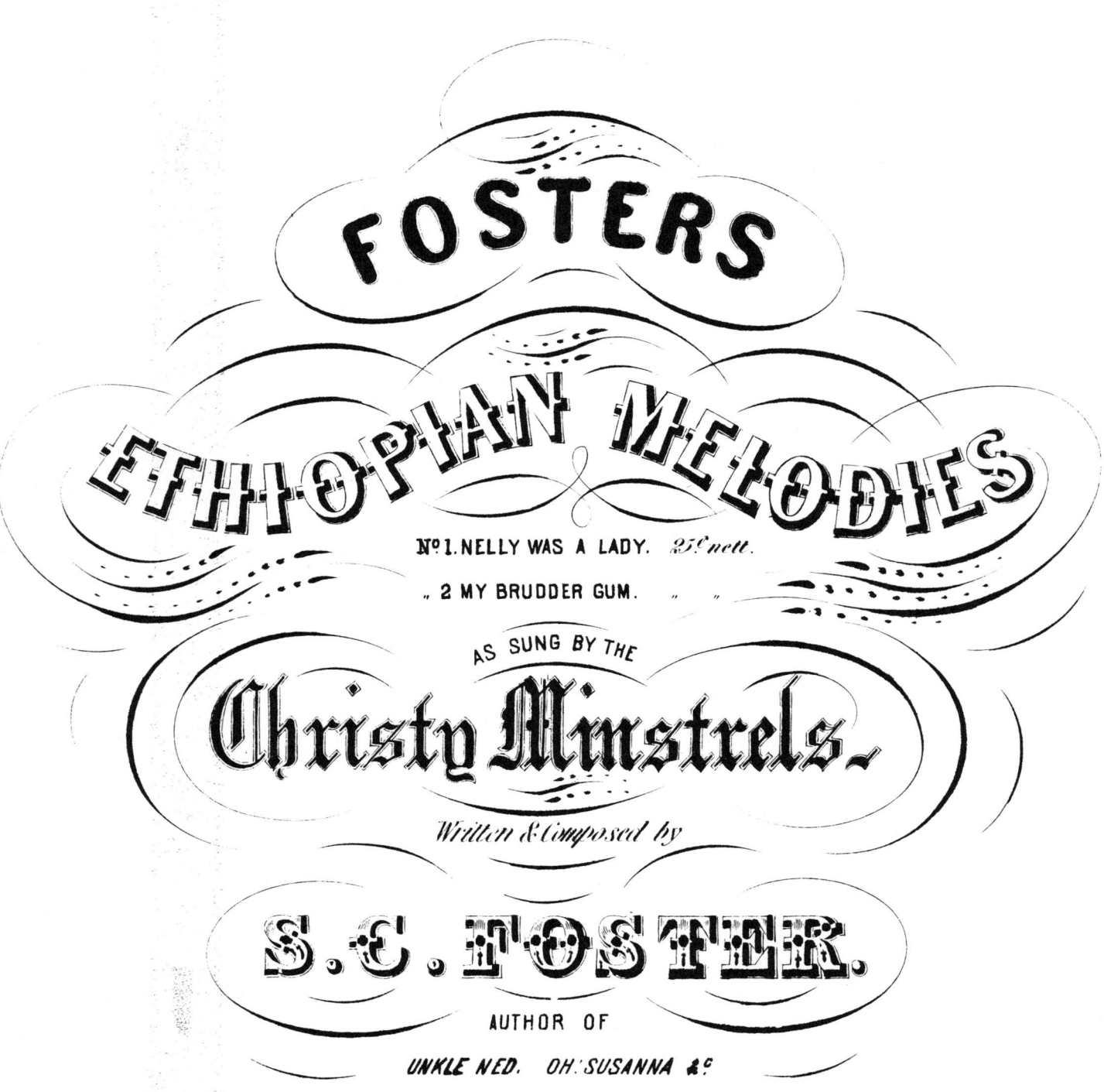

FOSTERS ETHIOPIAN MELODIES

Nº 1. NELLY WAS A LADY. 25¢ nett.

„ 2 MY BRUDDER GUM. „ „

AS SUNG BY THE

Christy Minstrels.

Written & Composed by

S. C. FOSTER.

AUTHOR OF

UNKLE NED. OH! SUSANNA &c.

Nº 3 DOLCY JONES 25 Cts. nett.   NELLY BLY 25 Cts. nett.

NEW YORK.

Published by FIRTH. POND & Cº. Nº 1 Franklin Sq.

NELLY BLY

Words and Music by S. C. FOSTER.

MODERATO.

Nelly Bly! Nelly Bly! bring de broom a_long, We'll

sweep de kitchen clean, my dear, and hab a little song. Poke de wood, my lady lub, And

make de fire burn, And while I take de banjo down, Just gib de mush a turn.

Heigh! Nelly Ho! Nelly, listen lub to me, I'll sing for you play for you, a

dulcem me_lo_dy. Heigh! Nelly, Ho! Nelly, listen lub to me, I'll

sing for you, play for you a dulcem me_lo_dy.

2d Verse.
Nelly Bly hab a voice like de turtle-dove, I hears it in de meadow and I hears it in de grove Nelly Bly hab a heart warm as cup ob tea, And bigger dan de sweet potato down in Tennessee. Chorus.

3d Verse.
Nelly Bly shuts her eye when she goes to sleep, When she wakens up again her eye-balls gin to peep De way she walks, she lifts her foot, and den she brings it down, And when it lights der's music dah in dat part ob de town. Chorus.

4th Verse.
Nelly Bly! Nelly Bly! nebber, nebber sigh, Nebber bring de tear drop to de corner ob your eye, For de pie is made ob punkins and de mush is made ob corn, And der's corn and punkins plenty lub a lyin in de barn. Chorus.

Quidor Engr.

FOSTERS

ETHIOPIAN MELODIES

Nº 1. NELLY WAS A LADY. 25ᶜ nett.

AS SUNG BY THE

Christy Minstrels.

Written & Composed by

S.C. FOSTER.

AUTHOR OF

UNKLE NED. OH! SUSANNA &c.

NEW YORK.

Published by FIRTH. POND & Cº *Nº 1 Franklin Sq.*

Entered according to Act of Congress AD 1849 by Firth Pond & Co in the Clerks Office of the Distᵗ Court of the Southⁿ Disᵗ of N.York.

NELLY WAS A LADY.

Written and Composed by

Stephen C Foster.

Down on de Mis-sis--sip-pi float-ing, Long time I trabble on de way,

All night de cot-ton-wood a to--ting, Sing for my true-lub all de day.

CHORUS

Nel_ly was a la_dy_   Last night she died,   Toll de bell for lub_ly Nell_ My

Nel_ly was a la_dy_   Last night she died,   Toll de bell for lub_ly Nell_ My

Nel_ly was a la_dy_   Last night she died,   Toll de bell for lub_ly Nell_ My

Nel_ly was a la_dy_   Last night she died,   Toll de bell for lub_ly Nell_ My

REPEAT CHORUS.

dark Vir_gin_ny bride.

dark Vir_gin_ny bride.

dark Vir_gin_ny bride.

dark Vir_gin_ny bride.

REPEAT CHORUS.

Now I'm un_hap_py and I'm weeping, Can't tote de cot_ton-wood no more;

Last night, while Nel_ly was a sleeping, Death came a knock_in at de door. CHORUS.

3rd VERSE.

When I saw my Nel_ly in de morning, Smile till she open'd up her eyes,

Seem'd like de light ob day a dawning, Jist 'fore de sun be_gin to rise. CHORUS.

4th VERSE.

Close by de mar_gin ob de wa_ter, Whar de lone weeping wil_low grows,

Dar lib'd Vir_gin_ny's lub_ly daughter; Dar she in death may find re_pose. CHORUS.

5th VERSE.

Down in de meadow mong de clober, Walk wid my Nel_ly by my side;

Now all dem hap__py days am o_ber, Fare_well my dark Vir_gin_ny bride. CHORUS.

"Nothing but a plain old Soldier"

Patriotic Ballad

Written & Composed by

STEPHEN C. FOSTER.

2½

NEW YORK

Published by JOHN J. DALY 419 Grand St.

Ent.d according to Act of Congress A 1863 by John J. Daly in the Clerks Office of the Dist. Court of the South.n Dist. of N.Y.

PEARSON N.Y.

I'M NOTHING BUT A PLAIN OLD SOLDIER

Poetry and Music by

STEPHEN C. FOSTER.

2. The friends I loved the best have de_parted, The days of my ear_ly joys have

1. I'm nothing but a plain old soldier, An old re_vo_lu_tion_ary

gone, And the voi_ces once dear And fa_miliar to my ear, Have

sol_dier, But I've handled a gun Where noble deeds were done, For the

fa_ded from the scenes of the earth one by one The

name of my com_man_ _ _der was George Washington. My

handled a gun Where no—ble deeds were done, For the

name of my com—man—der was George Washington.

3

Again the battle song is resounding,
 And who'll bring the trouble to an end?
The Union will pout, and Secession ever shout,
 But none can tell us now which will yield or bend.
You've had many Generals from over the land,
You've tried one by one and you're still at a stand,
But when I took the field we had one in command,
 Yet I'm nothing but a plain old soldier.
  CHORUS. Nothing but a plain &c.

Quidor, Engraver.

MUSIC OF THE ORIGINAL

CHRISTY

MINSTRELS,

THE

OLDEST ESTABLISHED BAND

in the

United States,

AS ARRANGED AND SUNG BY THEM WITH DISTINGUISHED SUCCESS

at all their

CONCERTS.

Edwin P. Christy.

NEW YORK.
Published by C. HOLT Jʀ 156 Fulton St.
BOSTON: OLIVER DITSON.

OH ! SUSANNA.

Sung by   Of the

G. N. CHRISTY,   CHRISTY MINSTRELS.

I came from Al _ a _ _ ba _ ma wid my ban _ jo on my knee, I'm g'wan to Lou _ si _ a _ na My true love for to see, It rain'd all night the day I left, The

come from Al _ _ a _ _ ba ma, wid my ban-jo on my knee.

come from Al _ _ a _ _ ba ma, wid my ban-jo on my knee.

come from Al _ _ a _ _ ba ma, wid my ban-jo on my knee.

come from Al _ _ a _ _ ba ma, wid my ban-jo on my knee.

2

I jumped aboard de telegraph,
And trabbelled down de riber,
De Lectrie fluid magnified,
And killed five hundred Nigger
De bullgine bust, de horse run off,
I realy thought I'd die;
I shut my eyes to hold my breath,
Susanna, dont you ery.
   Oh! Susanna - etc.

3

I had a dream de odder night
When ebery ting was still;
I thought I saw Susanna,
A coming down de hill.
The buckwheat cake war in her mouth,
The tear was in her eye,
Says I'm coming from de South,
Susanna, dont you cry.
   Oh! Susanna - etc.

4

I scon will be in New Orleans,
And den I'll look all round,
And when I find Susanna,
I'll fall upon the ground.
But if I do not find her,
Dis darkie 'I surely die,
And when I'm dead and buried,
Susanna, dont you cry.
   Oh! Susanna - etc.

Foster's Melodies

Nº 49.

OLD BLACK JOE

SONG

Written and Composed by

STEPHEN C. FOSTER.

Author of
FAIRY BELLE, GLENDY BURK &C.

2½

NEW YORK
Published by FIRTH, POND & CO. 547 Broadway.

Boston.
O. DITSON & CO.

Cincinnati,
C. Y. FONDA.

Pittsburgh,
H KLEBER & BRO

OLD BLACK JOE.

Poco Adagio

Written and Composed by S.C. FOSTER.

PIANO.

Gone are the days when my heart was young and gay, Gone are my friends from the cot-ton fields a-way, Gone from the earth to a bet-ter land I know, I hear their gen-tle voi-ces call-ing "Old Black Joe."

II. VERSE. Why do I weep when my heart should feel no pain
III. VERSE. Where are the hearts once so hap-py and so free? The

Why do I sigh that my friends come not a-gain,
chil--dren so dear that I held up-on my knee,

Griev-ing for forms Now de-par-ted long a-go? I
Gone to the shore where my soul has longed to go. I

hear their gen-tle voi-ces call-ing "Old Black Joe."
hear their gen-tle voi-ces call-ing "Old Black Joe."

FOSTERS AMERICAN MELODIES

Nº 21

OLD DOG TRAY

SUNG BY

Christy's Minstrels

Written & Composed by

STEPHEN C. FOSTER.

Nº 18. FAREWELL MY LILLY DEAR. Nº 19. MASSA'S IN DE COLD GROUND.
Nº 20. MY OLD KENTUCKY HOME, GOOD NIGHT.

25 Cts. nett.

NEW YORK
Published by FIRTH, POND & CO 1 Franklin Square.

Pittsburgh, H. KLEBER. Cincinnati, COLBURN & FIELD. WAKELAM & IUCHO St Louis

New Orleans, P.P. WERLEIN.

Wakelam.

Entered according to Act of Congress in 1853 by Firth, Pond & Co. in the Clerk's Office of the District Court of the Southern District of N.Y.

OLD DOG TRAY

Poetry and Music by

Sung by CHRISTY'S Minstrels.

S. C. FOSTER.

Andante, con Espressione.

The morn of life is past,   And evening comes at last;   It

brings me a dream of a   once happy day,   Of merry forms I've seen   Up-

on the village green,   Sporting with my old   dog   Tray.

CHORUS.

Old dog Tray's ever faith_ful, Grief cannot drive him a_way, He's

gentle, he is kind; I'll never, never find A better friend than old dog Tray.

3^{d.} Verse. When thoughts re_call the past His

The forms I call'd my own Have

eyes are on me cast; I know that he feels what my breaking heart would say: Al_

vanished one by one, The lov'd ones, the dear ones have all passed a_way, Their

though he cannot speak   I'll vainly, vainly seek   A better friend than old dog Tray.

happy smiles have flown, Their gentle voices gone; I've nothing left but old dog Tray.

Old dog Tray's ever faith _ _ ful,   Grief cannot drive him a_way;   He's

gentle, he is kind; I'll never, never find   A better friend than old dog Tray.

Quidor Eng.^{r.}

OLD FOLKS AT HOME

ETHIOPIAN MELODY

As Sung by

Christy's Minstrels

WRITTEN AND COMPOSED BY

E. P. CHRISTY.

Weller & Greene

25 ¢ nett.

NEW YORK *Published by* FIRTH. POND & CO. 1 Franklin Sq.

PITTSBURG. H. KLEBER.

Entered according to act of Congress in 1851 by Firth. Pond & Co. in the Clerks Office of the dist Court of the South.n dist of N.Y.

OLD FOLKS AT HOME

Words and Music by E. P. CHRISTY.

Way down upon de Swanee ribber, Far, far a—way,

Dere's wha my heart is turning ebber, Dere's wha de old folks stay.

Entered according to Act of Congress AD *1851* by Firth Pond & Co in the Clerks Office of the District Court of the South. Dist. of N.Y.

All up and down de whole cre‿ation, Sad‿‿ly I roam,

Still longing for de old plan‿ta‿tion, And for de old folks at home.

CHORUS.

All de world am sad and dreary, Eb‿ry where I roam,

Oh! darkeys how my heart grows weary, Far from de old folks at home.

2d. VERSE.

All round de little farm I wandered When I was young,

Den many happy days I squandered, Many de songs I sung.

When I was playing wid my brudder Hap — — py was I —

Oh! take me to my kind old mudder, Dere let me live and die.   CHORUS.

3d. VERSE.

One lit_tle hut a_mong de bushes, One dat I love,

Still sad_ly to my mem'ry rushes, No matter where I rove

When will I see de bees a humming All round de comb?

When will I hear de banjo tumming Down in my good old home?   CHORUS.

Quidor Eng.v.r

Old Folks at Home   103

MUSIC OF THE GREAT SOUTHERN

ORIGINAL   SABLE HARMONISTS   THE BEST BAND OF

SINGERS IN THE   UNITED STATES

ARRANGED & SUNG BY   AT ALL THEIR CONCERTS

LITH. OF E&S PALMER.

43 ANN ST. NEW-YORK.

New York, Published at MILLETS MUSIC SALOON 329 Broadway.

No.1 Old Uncle Ned   No.6 Lynchburg Town   No.10 Hard Times   Vo.14 Dandy Jim.
" 2 Roaring Riber.   " 7 Niggers History ob de World   " 11 Picayune Butler   " 15 Lucy Long.
" 3 Lousiana Belle   " 8 Susanna   " 12 Mary Blane   " 16 O Sally White

OLD UNCLE NED.

Written & Composed

For Wᵐ Rᵒᵒᵏ.

Of the

Sable Harmonists.

BY S.C. FOSTER OF CINCINNATI.

PIANO.

Dere was an old nig_ga dey calld him Uncle Ned Hes dead long a__go long a__go He had no wool on de top oh de head De place wha de wool ought to

Entered according to Act of Congress AD 1848 by W E Millet in the Clerks Office of the Disᵗ Court of the Southⁿ Disᵗ of N Y

grow.

And hang up de fid_dle and de

And hang up de fid_dle and de

Den lay down de shubble and de hoe_o__o And hang up de fid_dle and de

bow.   No more hard work for poor old Ned He's gone wha de good nig_gas go

bow.   No more hard work for poor old Ned He's gone wha de good nig_gas go

bow.   No more hard work for poor old Ned He's gone wha de good nig_gas go

His fingers were long like de cane in de brake

He had no eyes for to see

He had no teeffe to eat de oae cake

Se he had to luf dat oae cake he.

    Den lay down &c.

On a cold frosty morning poor Uncle Ned died

Masters tears down his cheeks ran like rain

Case he knew when poor Ned was under de ground

Hed neber see his like again

    Den lay down &c.

OPEN THY LATTICE LOVE

Composed for and dedicated

TO

MISS SUSAN E. PENTLAND

OF PITTSBURGH.

BY

L. C. FOSTER.

Lines from the New Mirror.

Philadelphia George Willig 171 Chesnut S.t

Allegretto.

PIANO.

delicatamente.

Open thy lattice love Listen to me! The cool balmy breeze is a _ broad on the sea! The

moon like a queen, roams her realms of blue, And the stars keep their vi_gils in

ral _ _ _ _ len _ _ _ _ tan _ _ _ _ _

heaven for you Ere morn's gushing light tips the hills with its ray, A _ way o'er the waters a _

_ way and a _ way! Then o pen thy lattice, love listen to me! While the moon's in the sky and the

breeze on the sea!

Open thy lattice, love listen to me!
In the voyage of life, love our pilot will be!
He will sit at the helm wherever we rove,
And steer by the load-star he kindled above
His shell for a shallop will cut the bright spray,
Or skim like a bird o'er the waters away;
Then open thy lattice &c.

RING DE BANJO

NEW ETHIOPIAN MELODY

WORDS AND MUSIC BY

S. C. Foster.

Author of "NELLY WAS A LADY", "NELLY BLY", ETC.

25 Cts. nett.

NEW YORK

Published by FIRTH, POND & CO, 1 Franklin Square.

New Orleans, WM. T. MAYO.

Entered according to Act of Congress AD 1851 by Firth Pond & Co. in the Clerk's Office of the District Court of the Southern District of New York.

RING, RING DE BANJO!

Words and Music by

STEPHEN C FOSTER.

3

Once I was so lucky,
  My massa set me free,
I went to old Kentucky
  To see what I could see:
I could not go no farder,
  I turn to massa's door,
I lub him all de harder,
  I'll go away no more.
    Ring, ring de banjo! &c.

4

Early in de morning
  Ob a lubly summer day,
My massa send me warning
  He'd like to hear me play.
On de banjo tapping,
  I come wid dulcem strain;
Massa fall a napping——
  He'll nebber wake again.
    Ring, ring de banjo! &c.

5

My lub, I'll hab to leabe you
  While de ribber's running high:
But I nebber can deceibe you——
  So dont you wipe your eye.
I's guine to make some money;
  But I'll come anodder day——
I'll come again my honey,
  If I hab to work my way.
    Ring, ring de banjo! &c.

Quidor Engᵛʳ.

FOSTER'S MELODIES Nº 29

SOME FOLKS

BY

S. C. FOSTER.

Author of

MAGGIE BY MY SIDE WILLIE WE HAVE MISSED YOU & C.

New York

Published by Firth, Pond & Cº *547 Broadway.*

Pittsburgh.
H. KLEBER.

Cincinnati.
W. F. COLBURN.

St. Louis.
W. W. WAKELAM

New Orleans
P. P. WERLEIN.

2½

SOME FOLKS.

Written and Composed by S.C. FOSTER.

Moderato.

Some folks like to sigh, Some folks do, some folks do;

Some folks long to die, — But that's not me nor you.

Long live the mer_ry mer_ry heart That laughs by night and day, Like the

Queen of Mirth, _ No mat_ter what some folks say.

2

Some folks fear to smile,

  Some folks do, some folks do;

Others laugh through guile, —

  But that's not me nor you.

    Long live the merry merry heart

      That laughs by night and day,

    Like the Queen of Mirth, —

      No matter what some folks say.

3

Some folks fret and scold,

  Some folks do, some folks do;

They'll soon be dead and cold, —

  But that's not me nor you.

    Long live, &c.

4

Some folks get grey hairs,

  Some folks do, some folks do;

Brooding o'er their cares, —

  But that's not me nor you.

    Long live, &c.

5

Some folks toil and save,

  Some folks do, some folks do;

To buy themselves a grave, —

  But that's not me nor you.

    Long live, &c.

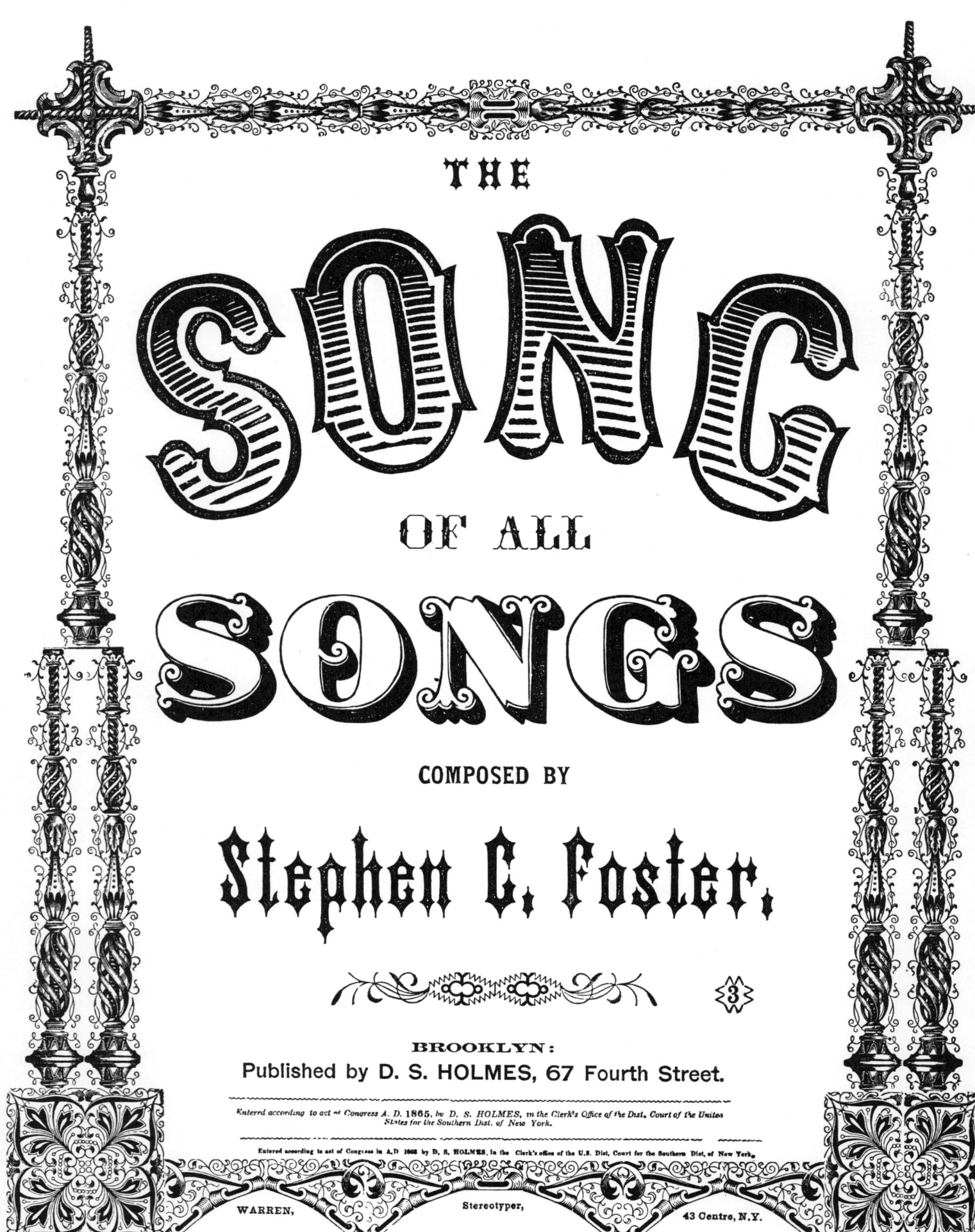

THE SONG

OF ALL

SONGS

COMPOSED BY

Stephen C. Foster,

3

BROOKLYN:
Published by D. S. HOLMES, 67 Fourth Street.

WARREN, Stereotyper, 43 Centre, N.Y.

THE SONG OF ALL SONGS.

Composed by STEPHEN C. FOSTER.

Moderato.

As you've walked through the town on a fine sum - mer's day, The

sub - ject I've got, you have seen, I dare say; Up - on fen - ces and rail - ings, where

ev - er you go, You'll see the pen - ny bal - lads stick - ing up, in a row; The

ti - tles to read you may stand for a while, And some are so odd, they will

cause you to smile; I no - ted them down as I read them a - long, And I've

put them to - geth - er to make up my song.

CHORUS.

Old songs! New songs! Ev - 'ry kind of song, I no - ted them down as I

read them a-long.

2.

There was "Abraham's Daughter" "Going out upon a spree,"
With "Old Uncle Snow" "In the Cottage by the sea;"
"If your foot is pretty, show it" "At Lanigan's Ball;"
And "Why did she leave him" "On the raging Canawl?"
There was "Bonnie Annie" with "A jockey hat and feather;"
"I don't think much of you" "We were boys and girls together."
"Do they think of me at home?" "I'll be free and easy still;"
"Give us now a good Commander" with "The Sword of Bunker Hill."

Chorus.—Old songs, etc.

3.

"When this Cruel War is over," "No Irish need apply,"
"For, every thing is lovely, and the Goose hangs high;"
"The Young Gal from New Jersey," "Oh, wilt thou be my bride?"
And "Oft in the Stilly Night" "We'll all take a ride."
"Let me kiss him for his Mother," "He's a Gay Young Gambolier;"
"I'm going to fight mit Sigel" and "De bully Lager-bier."
"Hunkey Boy is Yankee Doodle" "When the Cannons loudly roar,"
"We are coming, Father Abraham, six hundred thousand more!"

Chorus.—Old songs, etc.

4.

"In the days when I was hard up" with "My Mary Ann,"
"My Johnny was a Shoemaker," or "Any other Man!"
"The Captain with his whiskers" and "Annie of the Vale,"
Along with "Old Bob Ridley" "A riding on a rail!"
"Rock me to sleep, Mother," "Going round the Horn;"
"I'm not myself at all," "I'm a Bachelor forlorn."
"Mother, is the Battle over?" "What are the men about?"
"How are you, Horace Greeley," "Does your Mother know you're out?"

Chorus.—Old songs, etc.

5.

"We won't go home till morning," with "The Bold Privateer,"
"Annie Lisle" and "Zouave Johnny" "Riding in a Railroad Kerr;'
"We are coming, Sister Mary," with "The Folks that put on airs."
"We are marching along" with "The Four-and-Thirty Stars;"
"On the other side of Jordan" "Don't fly your Kite too high!"
"Jenny's coming o'er the Green," to "Root Hog or die!"
"Our Union's Starry Banner," "The Flag of Washington,"
Shall float victorious o'er the land from Maine to Oregon!

Chorus.—Old songs, etc.

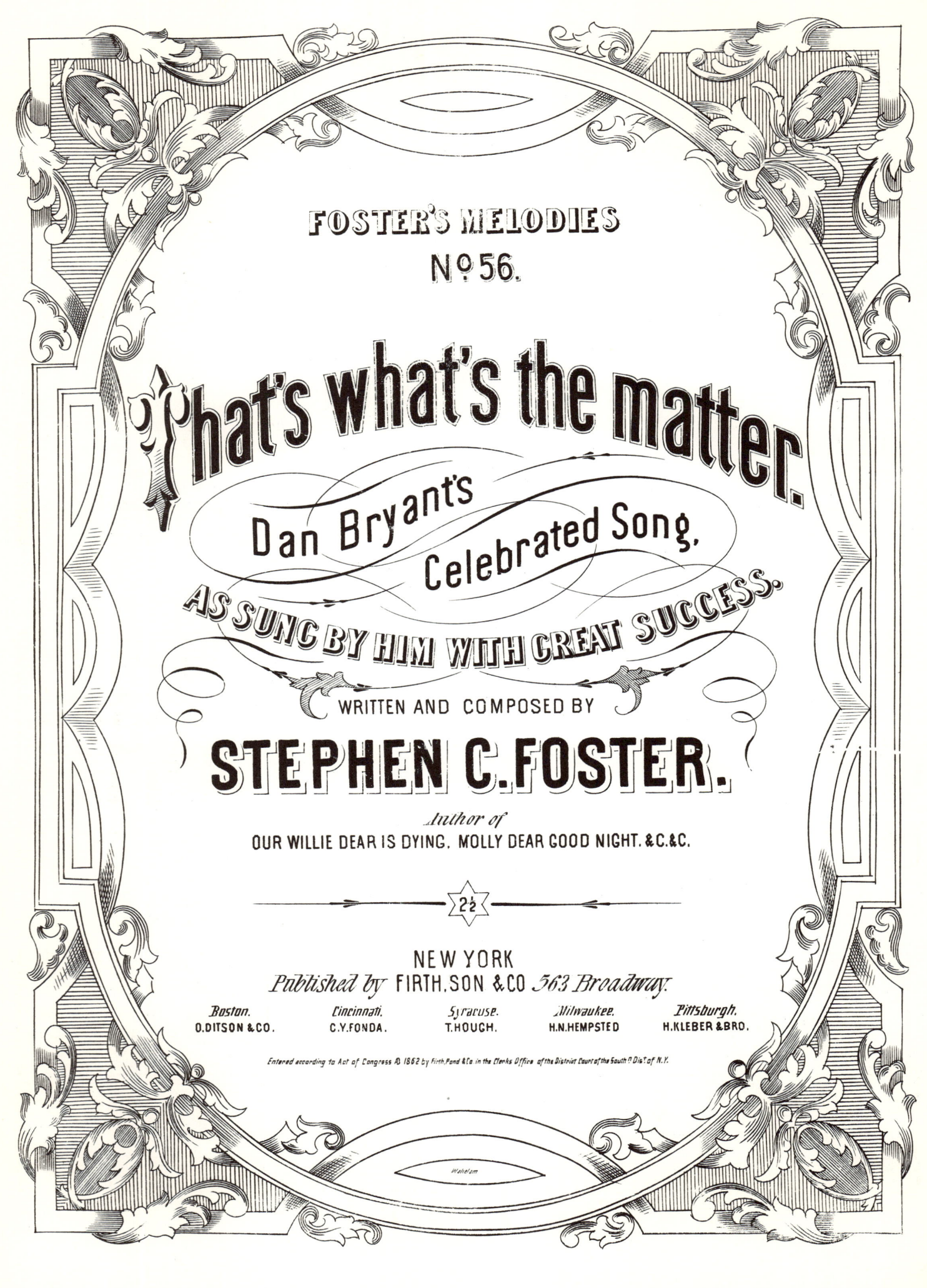

"THAT'S WHAT'S THE MATTER."

Words and Music
by
STEPHEN C. FOSTER.

MODERATO.

I. We live in hard and stir·ring times, Too sad for mirth, too rough for rhymes; For

II. Oh! yes, we thought our neigh·bors true, In · dulg'd them as their moth·ers do; They

songs of peace have lost their chimes, And that's what's the mat · ter! The

storm'd our bright Red, White and Blue, And that's what's the mat · ter! We'll

men we held as bro-thers true, Have turn'd in-to a reb-el crew; So
ne - ver give up what we gain, For now we know we must main-tain Our

now we have to put them thro', And that's what's the mat-ter!
Laws and Rights with might and main; And that's what's the mat-ter!

CHORUS.

That's what's the mat - ter, The reb-els have to scat-ter; We'll

make them flee, By land and sea, And that's what's the mat-ter!

3

The rebels thought we would divide,
And Democrats would take their side;
They then would let the Union slide,
    And that's what's the matter!
But, when the war had once begun,
All party feeling soon was gone;
We join'd as brothers, ev'ry one!
    And that's what's the matter!
                CHO'S.

4

The Merrimac, with heavy sway,
Had made our Fleet an easy prey —
The Monitor got in the way,
    And that's what's the matter!
So health to Captain Ericsson,
I cannot tell all he has done,
I'd never stop when once begun,
    And that's what's the matter!
                CHO'S.

5

We've heard of Gen'ral Beauregard,
And thought he'd fight us long and hard;
But he has play'd out his last card,
    And that's what's the matter!
So what's the use to fret and pout,
We soon will hear the people shout,
Secession dodge is <u>all</u> play'd out!
    And that's what's the matter!
                CHO'S.

Eng^{v.d} at Clayton's.

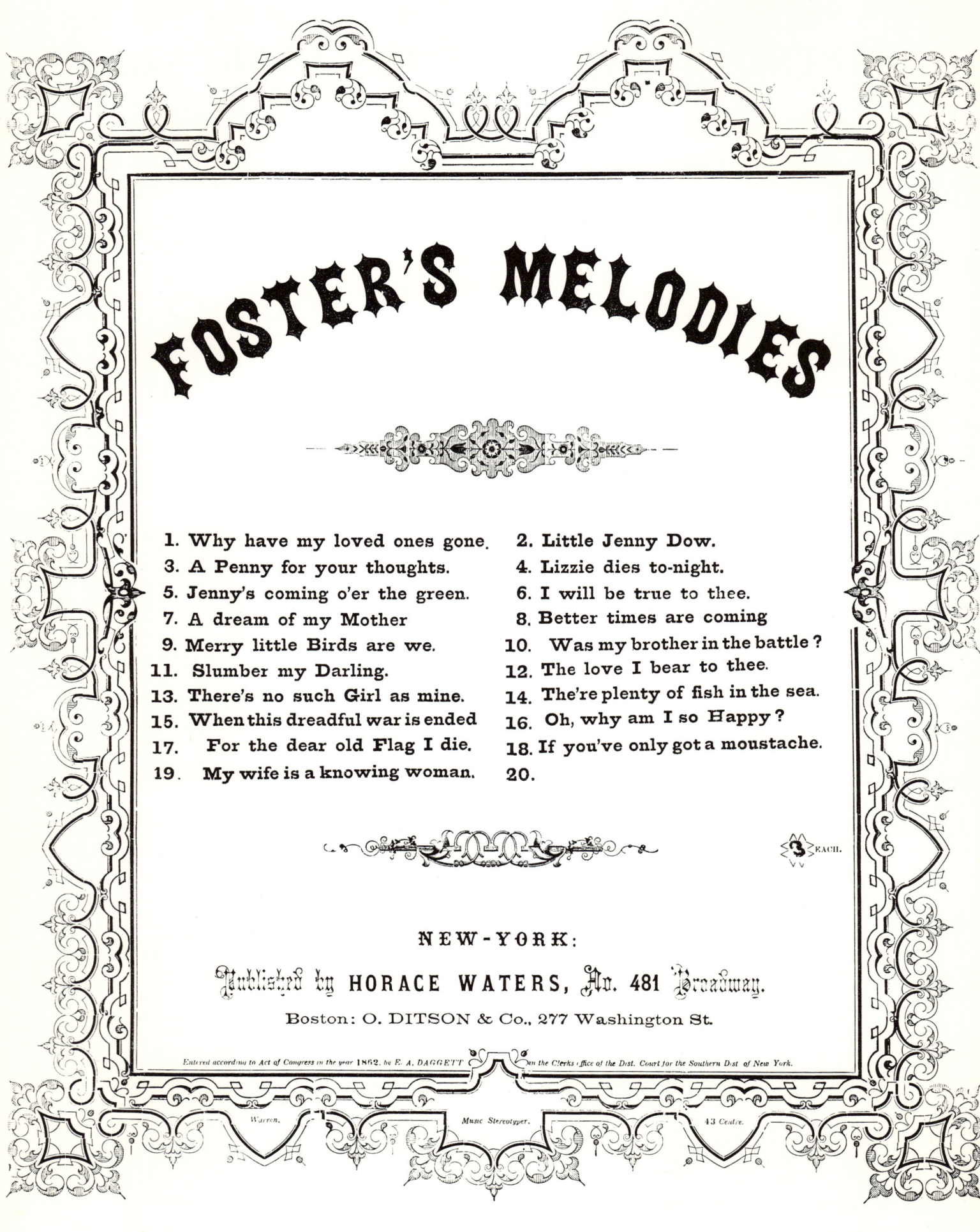

FOSTER'S MELODIES

3 EACH.

NEW-YORK:

Published by HORACE WATERS, No. 481 Broadway.

Boston: O. DITSON & Co., 277 Washington St.

Warren.   Music Stereotyper.   43 Centre.

THERE ARE PLENTY OF FISH IN THE SEA.

Written by GEORGE COOPER.

Composed by STEPHEN C. FOSTER.

VIVACE.

A la-dy tossed her curls At all who came to

woo; She laughed to scorn the vows, From

Entered according to act of Congress in A, D. 1863, by E. A. DAGGETT, in the Clerks office of the U. S. District Court for the Southern District of New York.

hearts   though false   or   true,   While   mer - ri - ly   she

sang ;   And   cared   all   day   for   naught,   There are

plen - ty   of   fish   in   the   sea,   As   good   as   ev - er   were

caught,   There   are   plen - ty   of   fish   in   the

sea,   As   good   as   ev - er were caught.

2.

Upon their lightning wings
   The merry years did glide,
A careless life she led,
   And was not yet a bride;
Still as of old she sang
   Though few to win her sought.
||:There are plenty of fish in the sea
   As good as ever were caught.:||

3.

At length the lady grew
   Exceedingly alarmed,
For beaux had grown quite shy
   Her face no longer charmed.
And now she sadly sings
   The lesson time has taught,
||:There are plenty of fish in the sea,
   But, oh, they're hard to be caught.:||

"THERE'S A GOOD TIME COMING"

SONG

Lines from the

London Daily News.

Composed for & Respectfully dedicated

TO

MISS MARY D. KELLER,

OF PITTSBURGH, BY

S. C. FOSTER.

Cincinnati. PETERS & FIELD — PETERS & WEBSTER *Louisville.*
New York, - FIRTH, HALL & POND, 239 *Broadway.*

There's a Good Time Coming

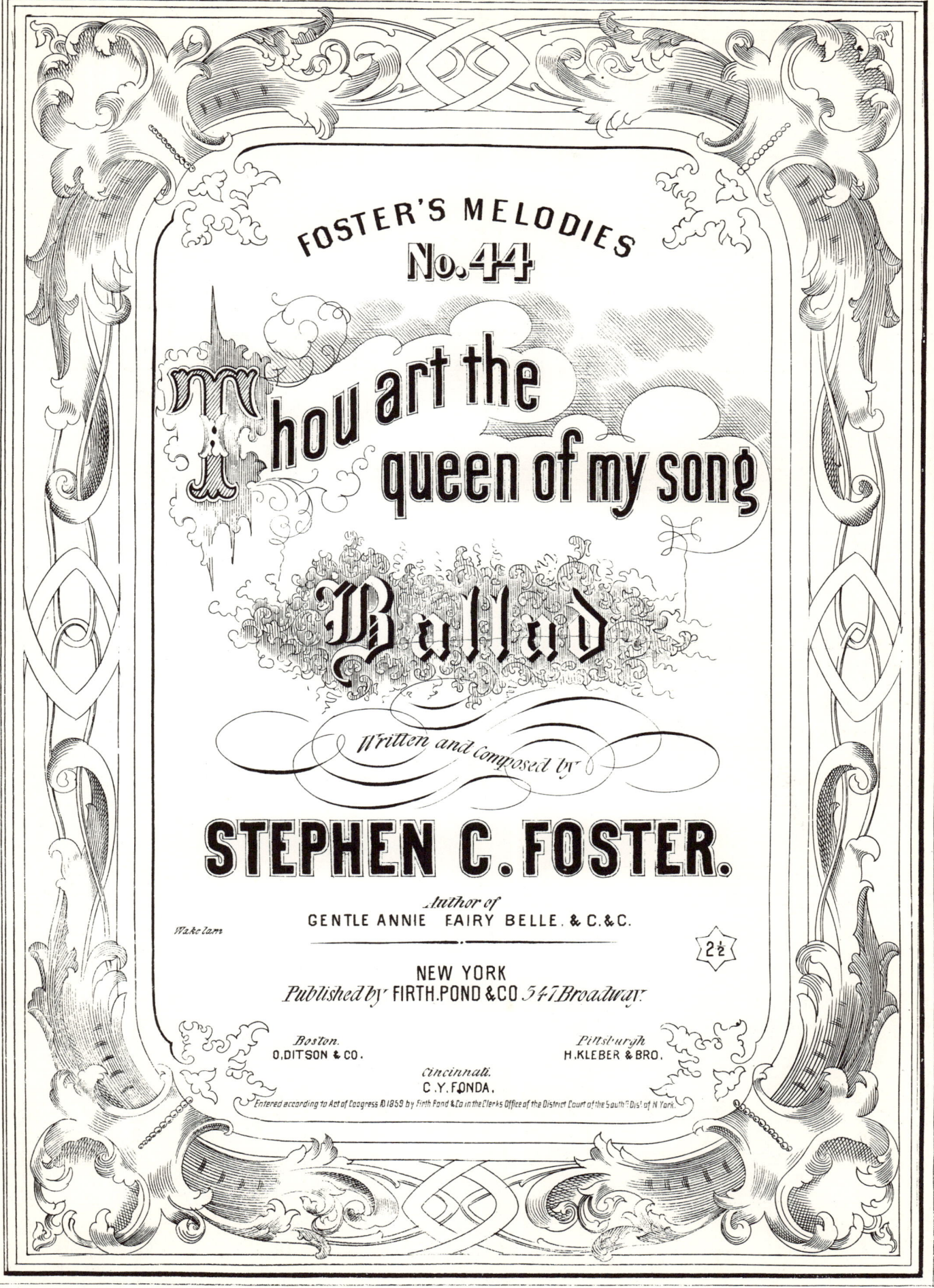

THOU ART THE QUEEN OF MY SONG.

POETRY & MUSIC BY STEPHEN C. FOSTER.

I. VERSE. I long for thee; must I long and long in vain? I sigh for thee; will thou come not back a_gain? Though

II. VERSE. The days are gone, days of summer bright and gay, The days of love we so fond_ly whiled a_way; But

III. VERSE. I turn to thee; though our hap_py hours have flown? I turn to thee; and my sad_dest thoughts are gone, For

ear _ _ ly years,   Thou art the queen of my song.
ear _ _ ly years,   Thou art the queen of my song.
ear _ _ ly years,   Thou art the queen of my song.

CRAVE PAR LAWSON

138   *Thou Art the Queen of My Song*

FOSTER'S MELODIES
Nº 30

THE
VILLAGE MAIDEN

Poetry & Music

BY

STEPHEN C. FOSTER.

Author of
COME WHERE MY LOVE LIES DREAMING, QUARTETTE. SOME FOLKS. ETC.

New York
PUBLISHED BY FIRTH, POND & Cº. 1 FRANKLIN SQUARE.

Rochester JOS. P. SHAW.
Pittsburgh H. KLEBER & BRO.

Buffalo J. SAGE & SONS.

W. F. COLBURN Cincinnati
W. W. WAKELAM. Sᵗ Louis.

THE VILLAGE MAIDEN.

POETRY AND MUSIC BY STEPHEN C. FOSTER.

The vil_lage bells are ring_ing, And mer_ri_ly they chime; The vil_lage choir is sing_ing, For

'tis a hap_py time; The chapel walls are la _ den With garlands rich and

gay, To greet the vil_lage maid_ en Up_on her wedding day.

2d VERSE. But summer joys have fa _ _ ded And

3d VERSE. The vil _ lage bells are ring _ _ ing, But

summer hopes have flown; Her brow with grief is sha _ ded, Her hap _ py smiles are
hark, how sad and slow; The vil _ lage choir is sing _ _ ing A requiem soft and

gone; Yet why her heart is la _ den, Not one, a _ las! can say, Who
low; And all with sor _ row la _ _ den Their tear _ ful tri _ bute pay Who

saw the vil _ lage maid _ en Up _ on her wedding day.
saw the vil _ lage maid _ en Up _ on her wed _ ding day.

TO

Miss Rebecca Wood.

THE
Voices that are gone

AS SUNG BY

WOOD'S MINSTRELS

WORDS BY

ROBT CAMPBELL ESQ.

MUSIC BY

STEPHEN C. FOSTER

The Symphonies and Accompaniments by
JOHN P. COOKE

3½

NEW YORK
Published by WM. A. POND & CO. 547 Broadway.

| Boston. | Buffalo. | Chicago | Milwaukee. |
| O. DITSON & CO. | J. R. BLODGETT. | ROOT & CADY. | H. N. HEMPSTED |

PEARSON

THE VOICES THAT ARE GONE.

STEPHEN C. FOSTER.

Lento e con espressione.

1. When the twi - light shades fall o'er me, And the ev - ning star ap - pears, Mem'- ry brings the past be - fore me, Joys and sor- rows, smiles and tears;

Then a-gain bright eyes are gleam-ing With the
love once in them shone, Then like mu - sic
heard when dream-ing, Come the voi - ces that are gone.

poco rit.

2.

Sweet as wood dove's note when calling
    To her mate as night draws on,
Soft as snow flake lightly falling
    Come the voices that are gone.
Voices heard in days of childhood
    Softly at the hour of prayer,
Or loud ringing through the wildwood
    When the young heart knew no care.
                Chorus.

3.

So when life's bright sun is setting
    And its day is well nigh done,
May there be no vain regretting
    Over memories I would shun;
But when death is o'er, to meet me
    May some much-lov'd forms come on,
And the first sounds that shall greet me
    Be the voices that were gone!
                Chorus.

heard when dream - ing, Come the voi - ces that are gone.

heard when dream - ing, Come the voi - ces that are gone.

(Eng⁴ at Clayton's.)

WAY DOWN IN CA-I-RO

Written & Composed

BY

STEPHEN C. FOSTER.

Author of NELLY WAS A LADY, DOLCY JONES, &c.

NEW YORK

Published by FIRTH, POND & Co. 1 Franklin Square.

Philadelphia, LEE & WALKER.   New Orleans, Wm T. MAYO.

"WAY DOWN IN CA—I—RO."

Written and Composed for

JAMES F TAUNT of the EMPIRE MINSTRELS

by STEPHEN. C. FOSTER.

Oh! la-dies dont you blush when I come out to play; I on__ly mean to please you all, and den I's guine a-way.

CHORUS.

RESPECTFULLY DEDICATED
TO THE PRESIDENT OF THE UNITED STATES.

WE ARE COMING FATHER ABRAAM

300,000

MORE

Music Composed

BY

STEPHEN C. FOSTER.

Price 25 Cts.

NEW YORK;
Published by S. T. GORDON, 706 Broadway.

Entered according to act of Congress A. D. 1862. By S. T. GORDON,, in the Clerk's Office of the District Court of the United States for the Eastern District of New York.

I. Hermann, Music Stereotyper & Electrotyper.   No. 199 William Street, New York.

WE ARE COMING, FATHER ABRAAM,

300,000 MORE.

SONG AND CHORUS.

By STEPHEN C. FOSTER.

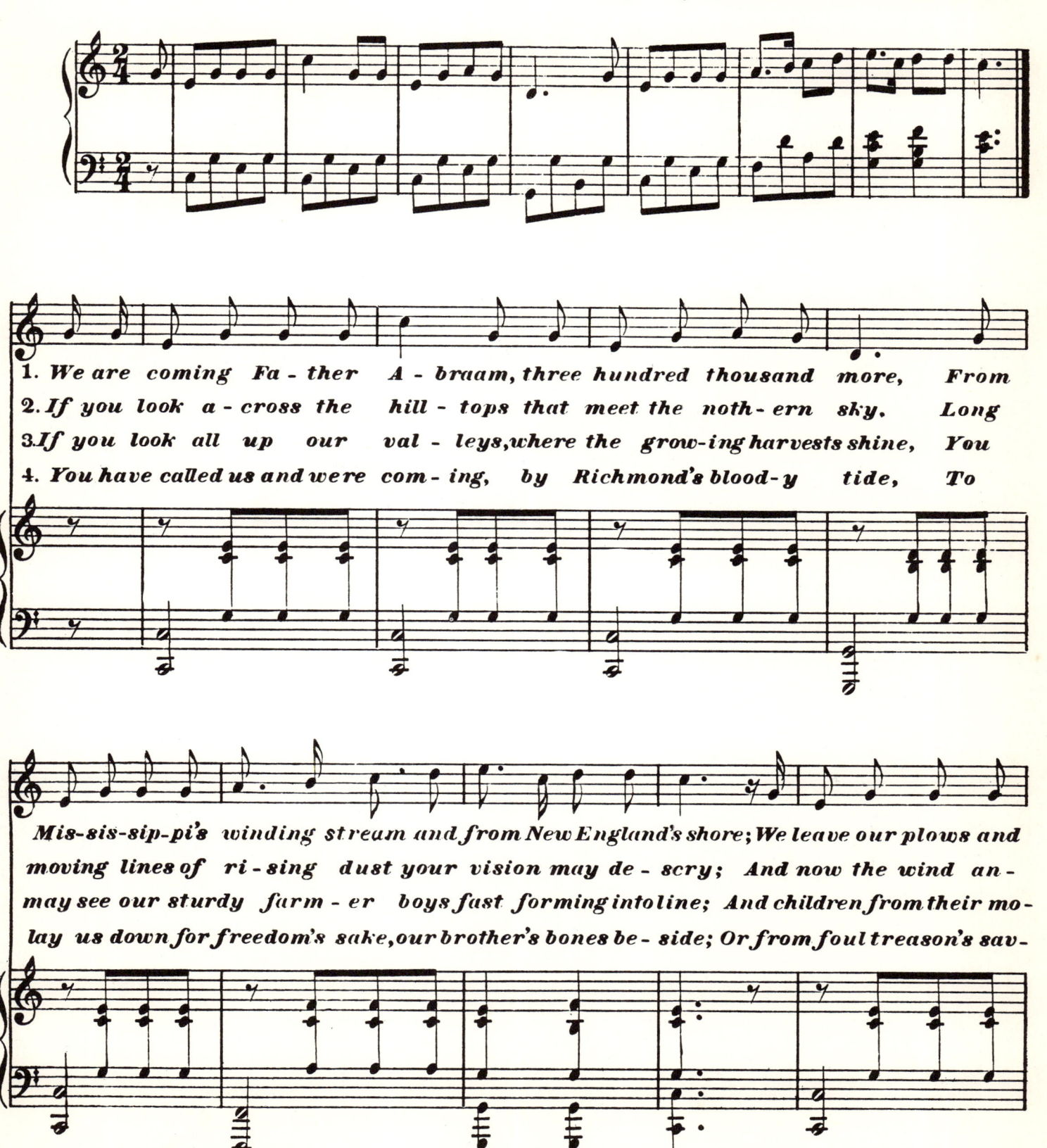

1. We are coming Fa - ther A - braam, three hundred thousand more,   From
2. If you look a - cross the hill - tops that meet the noth - ern sky.   Long
3. If you look all up our val - leys, where the grow-ing harvests shine,   You
4. You have called us and were com - ing, by Richmond's blood-y tide,   To

Mis-sis-sip-pi's winding stream and from New England's shore; We leave our plows and
moving lines of ri - sing dust your vision may de - scry; And now the wind an-
may see our sturdy farm - er boys fast forming into line; And children from their mo-
lay us down for freedom's sake, our brother's bones be - side; Or from foul treason's sav-

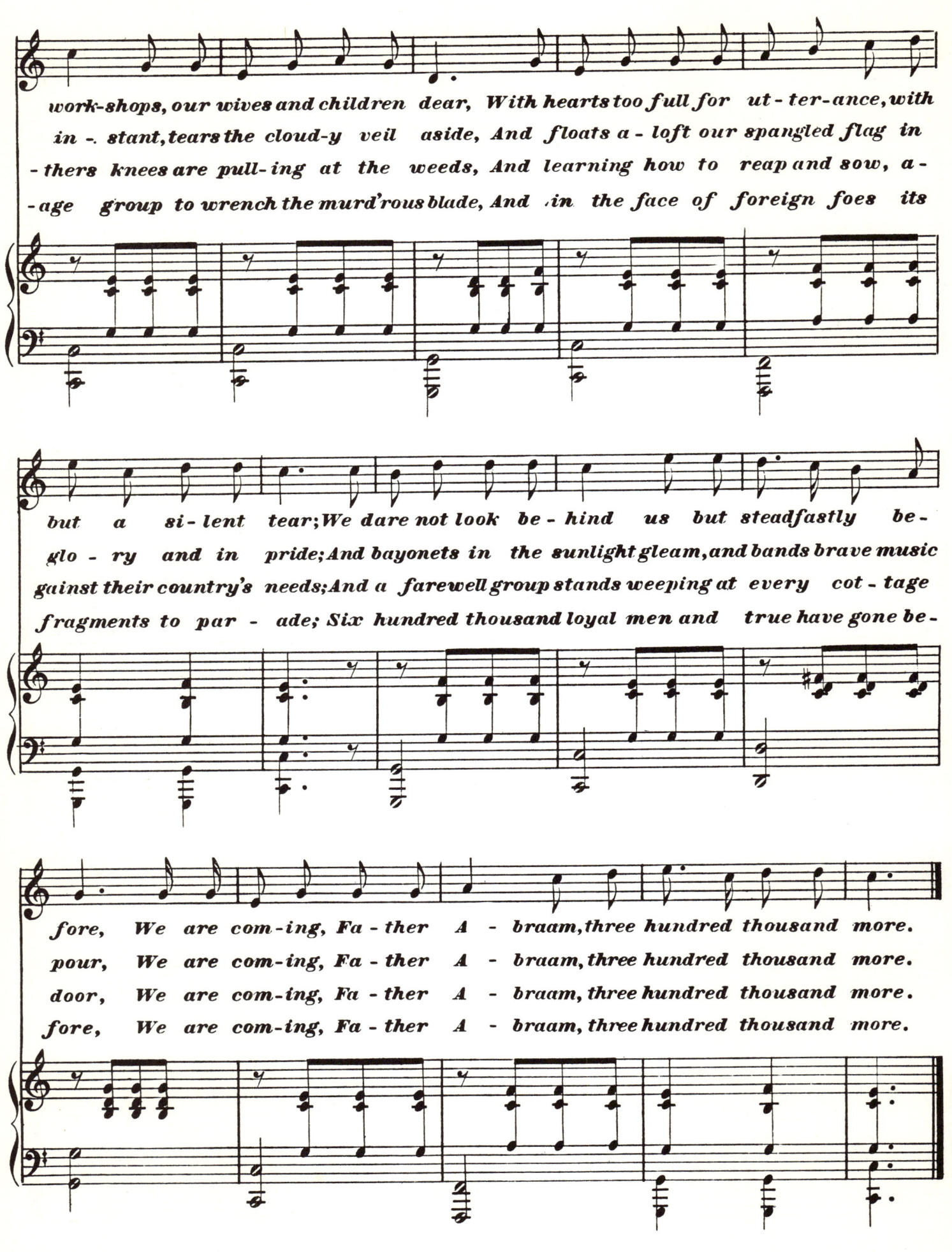

work-shops, our wives and children dear, With hearts too full for ut-ter-ance, with
in-. stant, tears the cloud-y veil aside, And floats a - loft our spangled flag in
-thers knees are pull-ing at the weeds, And learning how to reap and sow, a-
-age group to wrench the murd'rous blade, And in the face of foreign foes its

but a si-lent tear; We dare not look be-hind us but steadfastly be-
glo - ry and in pride; And bayonets in the sunlight gleam, and bands brave music
gainst their country's needs; And a farewell group stands weeping at every cot - tage
fragments to par - ade; Six hundred thousand loyal men and true have gone be-

fore, We are com-ing, Fa - ther A - braam, three hundred thousand more.
pour, We are com-ing, Fa - ther A - braam, three hundred thousand more.
door, We are com-ing, Fa - ther A - braam, three hundred thousand more.
fore, We are com-ing, Fa - ther A - braam, three hundred thousand more.

CHORUS.

We are com-ing, com-ing our union to re-store We are

com-ing, Fa-ther Abraam, with three hundred thousand more.

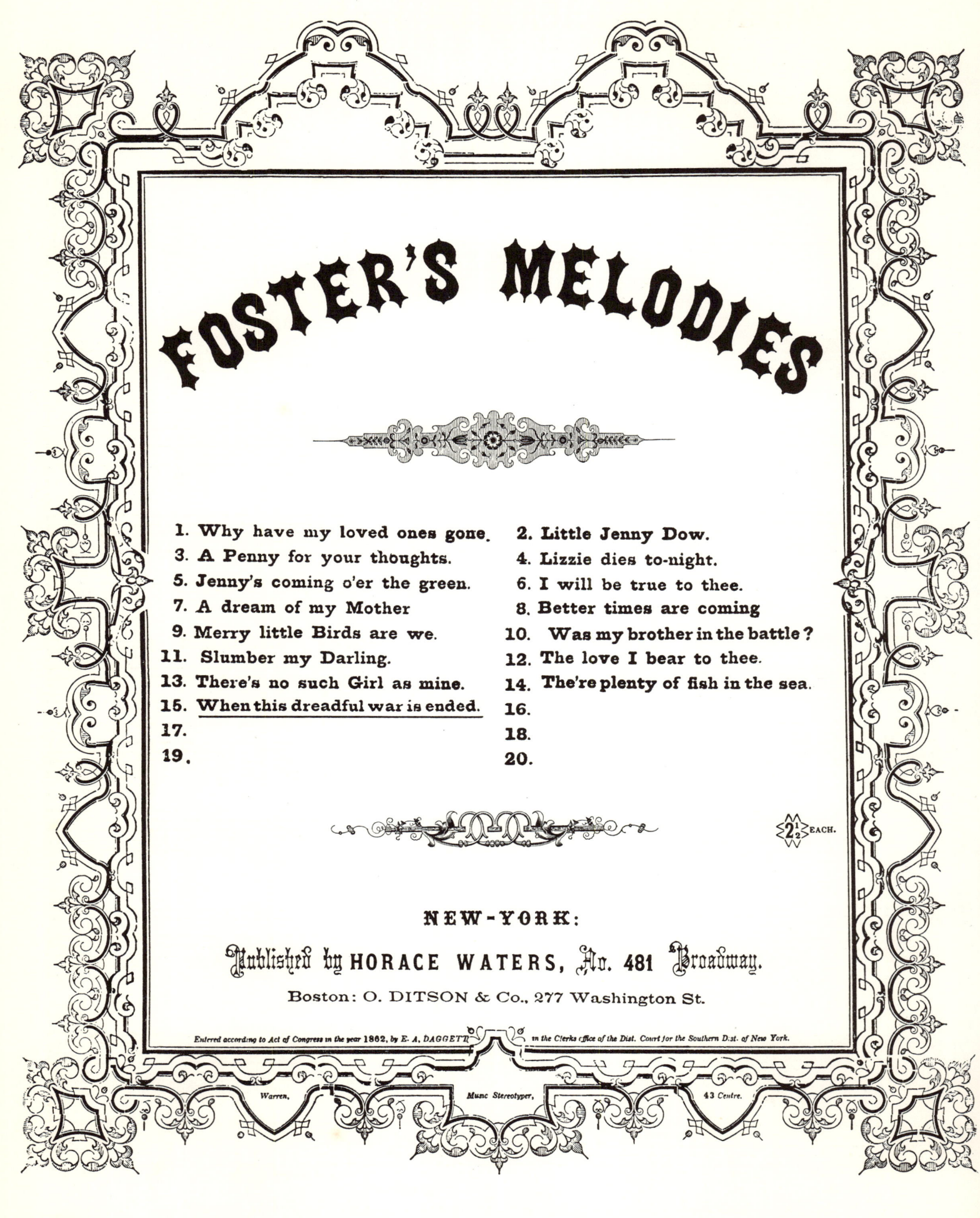

FOSTER'S MELODIES

1. Why have my loved ones gone.   2. Little Jenny Dow.
3. A Penny for your thoughts.   4. Lizzie dies to-night.
5. Jenny's coming o'er the green.   6. I will be true to thee.
7. A dream of my Mother   8. Better times are coming
9. Merry little Birds are we.   10. Was my brother in the battle?
11. Slumber my Darling.   12. The love I bear to thee.
13. There's no such Girl as mine.   14. The're plenty of fish in the sea.
15. When this dreadful war is ended.   16.
17.   18.
19.   20.

2½ EACH.

NEW-YORK:

Published by HORACE WATERS, No. 481 Broadway.

Boston: O. DITSON & Co., 277 Washington St.

Entered according to Act of Congress in the year 1862, by E. A. DAGGETT in the Clerks office of the Dist. Court for the Southern Dist. of New York.

Warren,   Munc Stereotyper,   43 Centre.

WHEN THIS DREADFUL WAR IS ENDED.

Written by GEORGE COOPER.

Music by STEPHEN C. FOSTER.

MODERATO, CON ESPRESSIONE.

1. When this dread-ful war is en-ded, I will come a-gain to you, Tell me dear-est ere we se-ver, Tell me, tell me you'll be true. Though to oth-er scenes I

CHORUS, *Cheerfully.*

TENOR.
How hap-py I will feel if I but know That you'll con-ten-ted be, I'll

SOPRANO.

ALTO.
How hap-py I will feel if I but know That you'll con-ten-ted be, I'll

BASS.

ne - ver, ne - ver have one pang of woe, Whi!e you are true to me.

ne - ver, ne - ver have one pang of woe, Whi!e you are true to me.

2.

On the gory field of battle
　　Your sweet voice will nerve my hand,
And when weary, sad or wounded
　　Your fair image near me stand.
In my visions, like some angel,
　　You will turn my grief to bliss;
On my pale and fevered forehead
　　I will often feel your kiss.
Our dear native land's in danger
　　And we'll calmly bide the time
'Till this dreadful war is over,
　　And the bells of peace shall chime.
　　　　Cho,—How happy I will feel, &c.

3.

When this dreadful war is ended,
　　(Soon I hope the day will come,)
Love's own star will lead my footsteps
　　Safely back to you and home.
Oh ! what joy again to meet you
　　When the threat'ning storm is past,
And the flag our foes have planted
　　Flies in shreds upon the blast
Farewell ! farewell ! best and dearest,
　　Do not let your heart repine,
Though the sky may now look gloomy
　　Soon the sun will brightly shine.
　　　　Cho.—How happy, &c.

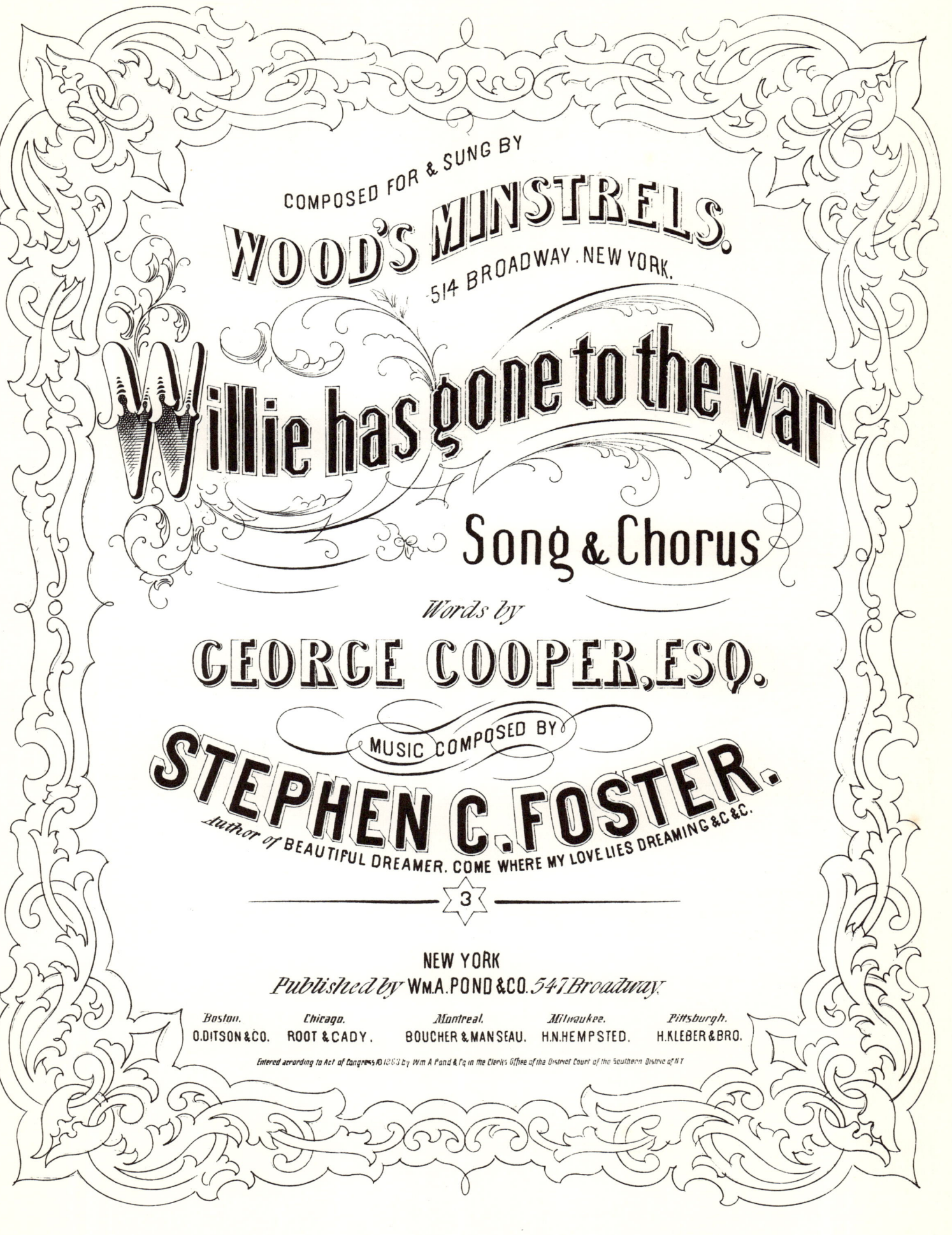

"WILLIE HAS GONE TO THE WAR."

Words by GEORGE COOPER.

Music by STEPHEN C. FOSTER.

Moderato.

I. The blue bird is sing- ing his
II. 'Twas here, where the li - ly bells
III. The leaves of the fo - rest will

lay,   To all the sweet flow'rs of the dale,   The wild bee is roam - ing at
grow,   I last saw his no - ble young face,   And now while he's gone to the
fade,   The ro - ses will with-er and die,   But spring to our home in the

Wil · lie my lov'd one is gone!

Wil · lie my lov'd one is gone!

Clayton.

TO MISS JULIA N. MURRAY.

WILT THOU BE GONE LOVE

VOCAL DUETT

SUBJECT FROM SHAKSPEARE'S

Romeo and Juliet

COMPOSED BY

STEPHEN C. FOSTER.

NEW YORK

Published by FIRTH, POND & Cº 547 Broadway.

Pittsburg R.H.KLEBER.   Louisville PETERS,WEBB & Cº

Entered according to Act of Congress A.D. 1851 by Firth, Pond & Cº in the Clerk's Office of the Dist. Court of the South. Dist. of New York.

WILT THOU BE GONE, LOVE?

JULIET. Wilt thou be gone, wilt thou be gone, love, gone, love, from me?

Stay! 'tis the Nightingale that sings in yonder tree. Deem not 'tis the Lark, love;

day is not yet near.___ Be-lieve me, 'tis the Nightingale whose song hath pierced thine

ear. Wilt thou be gone, wilt thou be gone, love, wilt thou be gone from me?

ritard tempo.

ROMEO. I must be gone, love, I must be gone from thee.

ritard f tempo.

Stay! 'tis the Nightingale that sings in yonder tree.   Love, 'tis the Nightingale,

'Tis not the Nightingale that sings in yonder tree. 'Tis the Lark,   'tis the

love, 'tis the Nightingale, love, 'tis the Nightingale that sings in yonder tree. Wilt thou be

Lark,   'tis the Lark, 'tis the Lark, love, that sings in yonder tree. I must be

gone, wilt thou be gone, love, gone, love, from me ___ gone, love, from

gone, I must be gone, love, gone, love, from thee ___ gone, love, from

me? ___

thee ___

Foster's Melodies. Nº 49.

OLD BLACK JOE.

DAN BRYANT.

Song & Chorus,
written & composed by
STEPHEN C. FOSTER.

Pictorial cover from an early edition of "Old Black Joe."

Notes on the Music

In general, the songs are discussed in alphabetical order by title (as the songs themselves are arranged in the book). Some songs, however, are discussed not in alphabetical order, but in relation with another, alphabetically occurring, song. For instance, in the first paragraph below, "Way Down in Ca-i-ro" is discussed along with "Ah! May the Red Rose Live Alway!" In such cases, an alphabetically occurring cross reference is supplied ("Way Down in Ca-i-ro": *see* "Ah! May the Red Rose Live Alway!").

1850 was a busy year for the twenty-four-year-old composer of "Oh! Susanna," already one of the most famous songs in America. During that year Foster made an important professional contact with Edwin P. Christy, the prominent minstrel-show entrepreneur; he married Jane McDowell; and he saw sixteen of his piano pieces and songs published. "Ah! May the Red Rose Live Alway!," the first song in this collection, and "Way Down in Ca-i-ro" were both brought out in April, the former by F. D. Benteen of Baltimore and the latter by Firth, Pond & Co. of New York. **Ah! May the Red Rose Live Alway!** is among the finest of Foster's earlier songs. His verses constitute a modest but perfectly acceptable lyric poem: it could be taken as the work of a reasonably talented minor Romantic poet—which is what Foster was, in his own way. The poem's nature images and its themes of innocence, beauty and mortality were to reappear throughout his work.

> Why should the beautiful ever weep?
> Why should the beautiful die?
>
> Why should the innocent hide their heads?
> Why should the innocent fear?

—these were the kinds of questions which were not only generally fashionable among poetically inclined mid-Victorian Americans; they seemed to have a special personal significance to the beautiful dreamer in their midst. If Foster perhaps drew from his own experience the substance of his melancholy reveries on vanished happiness and spoiled innocence, he pinpointed at least one area of the American experience of his day. Other areas—darker, more profoundly disturbing—were being explored by Edgar Allan Poe and other contemporaries. **"Way Down in Ca-i-ro,"** the other song of April 1850, is the composer strutting on the minstrel stage. It has a tonic effect: he is bright, clever, amusing, untroubled. He is the composer of "Oh! Susanna" and "Camptown Races" in fine form. The song is instructive as well as entertaining; it indicates the correct regional pronunciation of Cairo (rhymes with pharaoh), Illinois, as opposed to Cairo, Egypt.

"Beautiful Dreamer" was copyrighted and published in 1864 after Foster's death on January 13 of that year. The copyright date at the bottom of the first page of music in the first edition, however, is 1862, which suggests that the song was composed and prepared for publication in that year. This weakens the claim of the title page that "Beautiful Dreamer" was the "last song ever written" by Foster, "composed but a few days previous to his death." Furthermore, several of the twenty-odd songs published posthumously bore similar claims. It is not known for sure which song was actually Foster's last. Certainly "Beautiful Dreamer" is the most famous of the later pieces and is among Foster's most memorable sentimental ballads.

Of the seventeen Foster songs published in 1862, five reflect the greatest issue of the day—the Civil War. All of Foster's war songs espouse the Union cause, even though he apparently had no great liking for the current Republican administration. At this time, however, he was concerned with turning out songs for quick sale, and New York was hardly the place to peddle anti-Union sentiments. **"Better Times Are Coming"** indicates that Foster must have kept up with developments in the war, at least through New York newspapers; scattered throughout its nine verses are references to some of the most important military and political figures of the moment. Its mood is basically optimistic, which might be a reflection of the widespread belief that the war was going to be a short affair. **"We Are Coming, Father Abraam, 300,000 More"** is perhaps Foster's one really touching song of the war. It is a felicitous setting of a popular poem of the day by James S. Gibbons. Perhaps it was the poem's image of Lincoln as a great father that moved the composer to produce one of the better pieces of his last troubled years.

"Camptown Races" was composed probably in 1849 in Cincinnati and was published by F. D. Benteen of Baltimore in February 1850. This firm had published pirated versions of "Oh! Susanna" and "Old Uncle Ned" in 1848 and early 1849, but by 1850 had entered into a formal arrangement with the composer. During the latter year Benteen issued ten new Foster pieces. As can be seen from the original title page, the song was released as "Gwine to Run All Night, or De Camptown Races." It was the latter phrase, however, which rapidly caught the public's imagination and became the popular title. As soon as 1852, Benteen published a second edition of the song, this time with guitar accompaniment and a title page that read: "The celebrated Ethiopian Song/Camptown Races." The physical setting of the horse races detailed in the song is the kind of community that sprang up on the outskirts of frontier cities in the mid-nineteenth century. Here the Negro laborers and transients lived in shanties and tents —a camptown. Perhaps Foster visited such places in Cincinnati or Pittsburgh or heard the stevedores singing (or complaining) about them on the waterfronts. In any case, his dialect verses have all the wild exaggeration and rough charm of a real folk tale as well as some of his most vivid imagery:

> Old muley cow come on to de track . . .
> De bob-tail fling her ober his back . . .
> Den fly along like a rail-road car . . .
> Runnin' a race wid a shootin' star . . .

Foster quite carefully tailored the song for use on the minstrel stage. He composed it as a piece for solo voice with group interjections and refrain; he marked the score specifically:

> SOLO
>   De Camptown ladies sing dis song
> CHORUS
>   Doo-dah! doo-dah!

> SOLO
>   De Camptown racetrack five miles long
> CHORUS
>   Oh! doo-dah day!
>   etc.

The tune is an ideal vehicle for syncopated banjo parts with a rhythm section of tambourines and rattling bones. Together with "Oh! Susanna," "Camptown Races" is one of the gems of the minstrel era.

"Come Where My Love Lies Dreaming" (1855) is the only work Foster composed in four vocal parts without piano accompaniment. The piece is identified as a "quartette" on the title page; above the staff on the first page of music, Foster further labels it a "Serenade, per voci sole" [*sic*]. The use of this last "fancy" phrase, coupled with the slightly high-flown poetry and a slightly operatic coda marked *Finale ad lib:*, give the piece an air of pretentiousness unusual with Foster. "Now," he seems to be saying, "I am high class." However, one has only to hear (or take part in) a good performance of "Come Where My Love Lies Dreaming" for its naïve pretensions to become almost endearing. We are in familiar territory after all: the classic Foster heroine—untouchable, eternally dreaming—and the unmistakable Foster melody, here expansive and imaginatively phrased. No collection representative of his most interesting work could possibly do without it.

"Don't Bet Your Money on de Shanghai" (1861) is Foster's last dialect comedy song that approaches the verve and imagination of "Oh! Susanna" and "Camptown Races." As in the latter song, the scene is a sporting event, in this case a cockfight. The big Shanghai rooster (so elegantly lithographed on the title page) has strange eating habits and is not a good fighter; the best money rides on the "little chicken in de middle ob de ring."

The South, as pictured in Foster's songs, is a dreamlike paradise of eternal sunshine, happiness and music. It is the home of all loved ones and friends; it is the source of all cherished memories. It is a land where even backbreaking labor in the fields and on the docks is somehow pleasant. It is the haven to which all long to return, either to live or to die. Two pieces of early 1860 provide different aspects of this picture: **The Glendy Burk,** a good-natured levee song, and **Down Among the Cane-Brakes,** a tuneful reverie on the death wish. The Glendy Burke (Foster omitted the *e* in his song) was an actual steamboat, built in 1851, that worked the Mississippi out of New Orleans. The title page presents a vignette of the approaching ship and the narrator of the song waiting on the bank with a bundle tied to a stick ("I'll take my duds and tote 'em on my back when de Glendy Burk comes down"). The narrator does not wallow in nostalgia for the southland; he has simply decided to return and has laid plans to do so. He finds life in the mid-West cruel and uncongenial ("dey work too hard . . . dey make me mow in de hay field here And knock my head wid de flail") and will return to carefree existence as a dockworker in New Orleans. Furthermore, he will leave no Susanna behind to cry: his "lady love," a Miss Brown, will accompany him to the "sunny old south," presumably to become a dependent. This optimistic comedy is in direct contrast to "Down Among the Cane-Brakes." Though the narrator here is also an unhappy immigrant from "the Mississippi shore," he has no plan for returning. Now apparently in a condition of complete stasis, perhaps brought on by northern winters, he can only meditate on his mother's death, on his "lovely one, Who like the rest has gone," and long for his own death. It is one of those richly self-pitying laments that Foster indulged in from time to time. The absence of dialect from the song (as with the superior "Old Black Joe," published later in 1860) may indeed be an indication that it carries a measure of direct personal expression, despite the usual pseudo-southern trappings.

Both **"Gentle Annie"** (the only Foster song published in 1856) and **"Gentle Lena Clare"** (1862) are fine sentimental ballads. The major difference between them is that the former concerns a dead girl and the latter a living one (a rare privilege in Foster songs). Annie is but one of "many That have bloomed in the summer of [his] heart" but whose "spirit did depart." In fact, the great majority of Foster's ladies are either asleep or dead. There are precious few who (like gentle Lena Clare) apparently remain alive and well at the song's finish. The fatality list is grim: Annie (of "Annie My Own Love"); "Cora Dean" (described as the fairest of all "Long Island's lovely daughters"); Ella (of "Little Ella's an Angel"); "Ellen Bayne"; "Eulalie" (the "bride of death, lost Eulalie"); Eva (of "My Loved One and My Own"); "Jeanie With the Light Brown Hair"; "Laura Lee"; Lena (of "Lena Our Loved One Is Gone"); Lizzie (of "Lizzie Dies Tonight"); Lula (of "Lula Is Gone"); Lula (of "Where Has Lula

Gone"); Mary (of "Where Is Thy Spirit, Mary"); Nell (of "Nell and I"); Nelly (of "Nelly Was a Lady"); "Virginia Belle." The memorable **"Jeanie with the Light Brown Hair"** (1854), "Floating like a vapor, on the soft summer air," is certainly the most famous of Foster's departed heroines, but Nelly is the liveliest. Her syncopated requiem, published in 1849, was heard on minstrel stages all over the country, hard on the golden heels of her fabulous sister Susanna. The chorus of **"Nelly Was a Lady"** briefly eulogizes her in terms that are matter-of-fact and unsentimental:

> Nelly was a lady,
> Last night she died,
> Toll de bell for lubly Nell,
> My dark Virginny bride.

"(The) Glendy Burk": *see* "Down Among the Cane-Brakes"

Besides "Come Where My Love Lies Dreaming" there are three other pieces from 1855 included in this collection: **"Some Folks,"** Foster's witty, tongue-in-cheek toast to the carefree life; **"The Village Maiden,"** a neatly contrived if conventional sentimental ballad; and **"Hard Times Come Again No More,"** a compassionate tribute to the poor and oppressed. Here Foster refrains from nostalgia and heavy sentimentality: he is meditating on a real and present concern. The poem itself is somewhat clumsy ("While we all sup sorrow with the poor" and "There are frail forms fainting at the door" are two particularly unfortunate inventions), but it has sincerity and touches of real pathos. There is a striking moment in the chorus when the poet changes from observer to participant and directly addresses "hard times" in the first person:

> Many days you have lingered around my cabin door,
> Oh! Hard Times, come again no more.

There is a most interesting story regarding the background of this song. Morrison Foster provided the following information in his biography of his brother Stephen:

> When Stephen was a child, my father had a mulatto bound girl named Olivia Pise, the illegitimate daughter of a West Indian Frenchman, who taught dancing to the upper circles of Pittsburgh society early in the [nineteenth] century. "Lieve," as she was called, was a devout Christian and a member of a church of shouting colored people. The little boy was fond of their singing and boisterous devotions. She was permitted to often take Stephen

to church with her . . . . A number of strains heard there, and which, he said to me, were too good to be lost, have been preserved by him, short scraps of which were incorporated in two of his songs, "Hard Times Come Again No More" and "Oh, Boys, Carry Me 'Long." (Morrison Foster, *Biography, Songs and Musical Compositions of Stephen C. Foster . . .* , Pittsburgh, privately published, 1896, p. 20)

This passage constitutes one of the few first-hand accounts of Foster's experience with authentic Negro music.

"If You've Only Got a Moustache," copyrighted in 1862 but published posthumously in 1864, is one of five songs in this collection which have words by George Cooper (1840–1927), a young New York friend of the composer during his last years. The other Cooper songs are "My Wife Is a Most Knowing Woman" (1863), "There Are Plenty of Fish in the Sea" (1862), "When This Dreadful War Is Ended" (1863) and, "Willie Has Gone to the War" (1863). All of these songs are topical, the latter two dealing with Civil War themes and the others with comic subjects popular at the time. Most of the twenty-three songs on which Foster and Cooper collaborated were written for quick sale to publishers or minstrel performers with no royalty arrangements. Though these late songs do not approach the overall quality of, say, those of the early 1850's, they do demonstrate that Foster retained his facility at setting verses to appropriate and graceful tunes. George Cooper later became famous as lyricist of the song "Sweet Genevieve" (1869). When an old man, he gave a vivid eyewitness account of Foster's last illness (published in Harold Vincent Milligan's *Stephen Collins Foster, A Biography,* New York, G. Schirmer, Inc., 1920). It was Cooper who identified Foster's body in the morgue at Bellevue Hospital and notified the Foster family.

"Jeanie with the Light Brown Hair": *see* "Gentle Annie"

Two of the four Foster songs published in 1852 are included here: the famous "Massa's in de Cold Ground" and the all-but-forgotten "Maggie By My Side." The first song was one of Foster's most popular during his lifetime and a top seller along with "Old Folks at Home" and "My Old Kentucky Home." It earned over nine hundred dollars for the composer within five years of its publication, which means that an enormous number of copies were sold. He received only a two-cent royalty on each copy. "Massa" and "Old Folks at Home" have the same musical structure. Their initial phrases are each repeated five times, beginning every line except one; both of these phrases end with an octave skip in the melody; the chord progressions are the same. Both are slow elegiac songs in dialect written for the minstrel stage. Yet, despite these similarities, each song has a most distinctive character. Apart from the texts, it is difficult to imagine one ever being mistaken for the other. This is the kind of subtle magic that was part of Foster's talent. He could use the same basic musical materials—changing a few notes, altering an emphasis here and there, varying slightly an accompaniment figure—and produce two pieces of individuality and quality. "Maggie by My Side" is unusual among Foster's works in that it is a sea song. The narrator is a sailor ("Here let my home be, On the waters wide: I roam with a proud heart") and the Maggie of the title is apparently the sailor's dog (women never lived on sailing ships, of course). Judging from the evidence, she is a large and protective companion: the sailor remains indifferent to "the storm raging 'round" his pillow as long as he has dear Maggie sitting by his side. The original manuscript of this charming song brought a handsome price in the marketplace, but the sale occurred long after Foster was able to benefit, one hundred and four years after his death. In 1968 the two-page manuscript was sold at auction in New York's Waldorf-Astoria Hotel for $4,500. At the time of its sale, the dealer described the item as "without doubt the most important American musical manuscript still in private hands." Foster's signature, let alone a complete song in his handwriting, is regarded by collectors as one of the rarest among famous Americans. Foster's most famous canine tribute is of course "Old Dog Tray," published a year after "Maggie." In this song the composer wedded one of his most graceful melodies with one of his most mawkish texts. Here again is a desolate character in the evening of life who has outlived everyone he ever cared about and has nothing left but his memories and an old dog. The animal is truly wondrous, however. He is not only faithful, gentle and kind; he can read minds ("When thoughts recall the past His eyes are on me cast") and feel human emotions ("I know that he feels what my breaking heart would say"). He is, in short, a man's best friend: "Although he cannot speak . . . I'll never, never find A better friend than old dog Tray."

"My Old Kentucky Home, Good Night" was composed probably in 1852 and was published in January 1853. There are several legends which connect the famous song to Federal Hill, the summer home of Judge John Rowan in Bardstown, Kentucky, but there is no documentary evidence from the period to prove that Foster had much connection with the place. Judge Rowan, at one time United States Senator from Kentucky, was a cousin of Stephen's father and well known to the Foster family. Charlotte and Ann Eliza Foster, two of Stephen's sisters, visited Federal Hill in the late 1820's, Charlotte receiving (but rejecting) a marriage proposal from John Rowan, Jr. Stephen probably visited Federal Hill in the 1840's, but it is most unlikely that he composed "My Old Kentucky Home" there or that he even had the house in mind when he composed it. Foster's manuscript workbook reveals that the original title of the poem was "Poor Uncle Tom, Good Night" and that the text varied from that of the final published version. Each verse originally ended with the line "Den poor Uncle Tom, good night." Foster was perhaps attempting to capitalize on Harriet Beecher Stowe's recently published best-seller *Uncle Tom's Cabin* (1851–2) rather than celebrating his relative's old Kentucky home. Nevertheless, legends die hard. Federal Hill is still secure in Foster lore and is a museum and tourist attraction. Kentucky took the song as its own long ago and finally proclaimed it the official state song in 1928. And with good reason: it is certainly the most famous song about the state (regardless of what Foster did or did not have in his mind when he wrote it) and is one of the composer's most appealing nostalgia pieces. It can be a moving experience to witness the traditional ritual at the opening of the annual Kentucky Derby in Louisville when the thousands of spectators rise and sing "My Old Kentucky Home" with a fervor and solemnity occasionally reserved for the national anthem.

"My Wife Is a Most Knowing Woman"; *see* "If You've Only Got a Moustache"

"Nelly Bly" danced her way on stage with Christy's Minstrels in 1850 and remained a popular favorite for many years. One can imagine it as a song for two kitchen maids (the chorus is set for only two female voices) who sing and play the banjo as they attend their chores of sweeping, stoking the fire and preparing food.

"Nelly Was a Lady": *see* "Gentle Annie"

The hero of **"Nothing But a Plain Old Soldier"** (1863) is not a member of the Union army, as might be expected; he is a veteran of the revolutionary war who fought under George Washington. This centenarian muses for two verses about his past ("I've handled a gun Where noble deeds were done"), his dead friends and relatives, and about his longing for death—all the usual preoccupations of Foster characters. But the real *raison d'être* of the song is revealed in the last verse. It is Foster's own lightly cynical comment on the Civil War at the end of its second year. Perhaps the publisher was a bit uneasy about this; the title page assures us in large type that the piece is, after all, a "Patriotic Ballad." The label would have been more appropriate for **"That's What's the Matter,"** one of the Foster war songs published the year before. It expresses conventional anti-Confederate sentiments and is cast as a spirited minstrel piece (though no dialect is used). At the end of the song Foster could blithely state:

> So what's the use to fret and pout,
> We soon will hear the people shout,
> Secession dodge is *all* play'd out!

But at the end of "Nothing But a Plain Old Soldier" he parodied these lines, his optimism faded:

> The Union will pout, and Secession ever shout,
> But none can tell us now which will yield or bend.

In overall cleverness of text and tune, "That's What's the Matter" is the better of the two songs. The title page calls it "Dan Bryant's Celebrated Song, as sung by him with great success." Foster was undoubtedly hoping that the famous minstrel's success with it would rival that of another "celebrated song"—the incredible "Dixie"— composed for Bryant three years earlier by Daniel D. Emmett.

"Oh! Susanna" was first performed in public on 11 September 1847 in Pittsburgh. The setting of the modest premiere (it was sung by a local quintette) was the Andrews' Eagle Ice Cream Saloon, undoubtedly a proper home for "Susanna's" zany contradictions and farce-comedy. Foster is said to have written the song for informal use by a men's social group of which he and his brother Morrison were members (he definitely wrote "Lou'siana Belle" and "Old Uncle Ned" earlier for this group). Within fourteen months of "Susanna's" first public hearing, at least eight different copyright claims for the piece were registered by publishers in New York, Massachusetts and Maryland. Foster's name appeared as composer on a few of these unauthorized versions but he received no remuneration whatsoever for them. This situation, however, was largely brought on by the youthful and inexperienced composer himself. In the 1840's he began to approach performers in the touring black-face minstrel shows, hoping to interest them in performing his early songs. He apparently handed out numerous manuscript copies to all who would accept them. Some of the copies passed into the hands of publishers eager for potential new hits "As Sung By the Christy Minstrels" or some other famous troupe. In this case, the song was widely known even before it came from the presses. If Foster ever received any money for "Oh! Susanna" it probably came from William C. Peters, a music dealer and publisher in Cincinnati who had published four of Foster's earliest songs. In an article written three years after Foster's death,* Robert Peebles Nevin stated that Peters asked for both "Oh! Susanna" and "Uncle Ned" and that the composer gave them to him without thought of receiving payment. (Nevin was a close friend of Foster in Pittsburgh and the father of two composers, Ethelbert and Arthur Nevin.) Peters published both songs in 1848 and, according to Nevin, gave the composer nothing for "Uncle Ned" and one hundred dollars for "Oh! Susanna." Both parties were reportedly pleased with the deal: Foster was convinced he could make real money as a songwriter (and in 1848 one hundred dollars *was* real money) while Peters eventually made ten thousand dollars on the two songs (and in 1848 this was an incredible fortune).**

Of all Foster's dialect songs, "Oh! Susanna" seems closest to being an authentic folk piece. Musically it has the snap and dash typical of so many regional banjo and fiddle tunes; textually it has the heady nonsense of an anonymous British ditty transformed by the rowdy American Frontier. Certainly the thousands of adventurers and homesteaders who immediately took "Susanna" with them to the West, eager for gold and land, made her their very own. She seems more suited somehow to their company on the trail than to that of the gentle young musician performing in the parlors of Pittsburgh and Cincinnati.

---

* Stephen C. Foster and Negro Minstrelsy," *The Atlantic Monthly* (November 1867).

** The sum Peters earned from the songs is reported by Morrison Foster, *Biography . . . of Stephen C. Foster . . .,* Pittsburgh, 1896, p. 13.

"Old Black Joe" was composed probably a short time before Foster moved permanently from Pittsburgh to New York in the later summer or early Fall of 1860. Among the select group of Foster's internationally famous songs, "Old Black Joe" (along with its relative "Old Uncle Ned") has perhaps become the most tarnished in its century of existence. Not only has the original been encrusted with merciless parodies; the central image of the song—the faithful old "darkey" servant—has been long since discredited as symptomatic of an attitude and a way of life both vicious and corrupt. Along with numerous other artefacts of popular culture, including the minstrel show itself, the song and its imitations were perhaps necessary casualties along the road to contemporary social awareness. Taken on its own terms, however, and especially within the context of the last four years of Foster's career, "Old Black Joe" can be judged a superior achievement. It has a directness of expression and a grace and naturalness of melodic line that place it near "Old Folks at Home" and his other finest sentimental ballads. The text is in Foster's own poetic language with no trace of dialect (he had not written expressly for the minstrel stage for about seven years). There may be more than a little of Foster himself injected into the song: with his mother, father and various other members of his family dead, with his marriage on shaky ground and his finances unstable, and with his drinking probably increasing, he could well have longed for former times when his "heart was young and gay" and could almost have heard the "gentle voices calling."

"Old Dog Tray": *see* "Maggie By My Side"

"Old Folks at Home," composed in Pittsburgh and published in New York in October 1851, was undoubtedly Foster's most popular song and the one that earned him (and later his widow and daughter) the largest royalties from sheet-music sales. It is the song that over a hundred and twenty years after its appearance is perhaps the most immediately associated with the composer's name. A long-noted irony in this respect is that Foster's name did not appear during his lifetime on the published song, as can be seen from the facsimile cover of the first edition included in this collection. (His name did appear as composer after the copyright of the song was renewed in 1879). It was of course E. P. Christy who was credited as having "written and composed" "Old Folks at Home," and Foster himself was responsible for this. He apparently sold to Christy the right to be publicized as composer of the song for the sum of $5.00. (Morrison Foster wrote in his 1896 biography of his brother that Christy paid $500.00 for the right, but this claim has been persuasively disputed by John Tasker Howard and other Foster authorities.) This did not affect in any way Foster's receipt of royalties on the song—his publisher was a party to the arrangement. Nevertheless, eight months after "Old Folks" appeared, the composer regretted his action and tried to nullify the agreement; on May 25, 1852 he wrote to Christy:

> As I once intimated to you, I had the intention of omitting my name on my Ethiopian songs, owing to the prejudice against them by some, which might injure my reputation as a writer of another style of music, but I find that by my efforts I have done a great deal to build up a taste for the Ethiopian songs among refined people . . . . Therefore I have concluded to reinstate my name on my songs and to pursue the Ethiopian business without fear or shame . . . . As it was at my own solicitation that you allowed your name to be placed on the song, I hope that the above reasons will be sufficient explanation for my desire to place my own name on it as author and composer . . . . This is a little matter of pride in myself which will certainly be to your interest to encourage. On the receipt of your free consent to this proposition, I will if you wish, willingly refund you the money which you paid me on that song . . . . I find I cannot write at all unless I write for public approbation and get credit for what I write.[*]

Christy was obviously unmoved by Foster's plea and the false credit was carried on the published music for the following twenty-seven years. In fact, Christy's name appeared in this manner on the songs of other composers of the day, among them Henry Clay Work. The fame of "Old Folks at Home" was rapid and widespread. It became known throughout the United States and in Europe (Christy's minstrel troupe brought it to England, where it was immensely popular). References to the song, both laudatory and damning, may be found in newspapers and journals of the day. Only one year after the song was published, the prestigious *Dwight's Journal of Music* (Boston) quoted a correspondent in Albany, New York:

> "Old Folks at Home" . . . is on everybody's tongue, and consequently in everybody's mouth. Pianos and guitars groan with it, night and day; sentimental young ladies sing it; sentimental young gentlemen warble it in midnight serenades . . . boatmen roar it out stentorially at all times; all the bands play it . . . the "singing stars" carol it on the theatrical boards, and at concerts . . . . (Oct. 2, 1852, p. 202)

A year later, *Dwight's Journal* published remarks by an editor who was obviously sick of hearing "Old Folks at Home" and horrified that "such tunes" were so insidious that even "deeply musical persons" hummed and whistled them involuntarily; he equated them with "a morbid irritation of the skin" (Nov. 19, 1853, p. 54). Such rumblings of displeasure from the musical establishment were fleeting, however, and Foster's sentimental, irresistible piece endured even its initial overexposure to become an American classic. During the 1890's, Antonín Dvořák chose to set "Old Folks at Home" for solo voices, chorus and orchestra as a gesture of affection for his temporary home. When he conducted it in New York, "it met with such instant appreciation that they had to play it through again."[*] The plantation scene of Foster's celebration of the good life among the old folks was originally set on the Pedee River. Drafts of the poem in his workbook (now in the Foster Hall Collection at the University of Pittsburgh) read:

> Way down upon de Pedee ribber
> Far far away

and then:

> Swanee
> Way down upon de ~~Pedee~~ ribber
> Far, far away

Both names were apparently picked at random from an atlas since Foster had no first-hand knowledge of the southern rivers. He undoubtedly decided to use the two-syllable corruption of Florida's Suwanee because the initial vowel is certainly more graceful for singing. It is hard to imagine what subsequent generations of Tin Pan Alley lyricists would have done without the corrupt but musical Swanee to fall back on. The word eventually served almost as well as the mythical Dixie to conjure a stereotyped southern setting. It is difficult to believe, too, that even a George Gershwin could have produced the hit song of 1919 if it had been named "Pedee" instead of "Swanee." "Old Folks at Home" was proclaimed the official state song of Florida in 1935.

[*] A facsimile of this letter is in Music Division, The New York Public Library. It is quoted in Gilbert Chase, *America's Music, from the Pilgrims to the Present*, rev. 2nd ed., New York, McGraw-Hill, 1966, pp. 293–4, and in John Tasker Howard, *Stephen Foster, America's Troubadour*, New York, Tudor Publishing Company, 1943, pp. 196–7.

[*] Paul Stefan, *Anton Dvořák*, New York, Greystone Press, 1941, p. 227.

"Old Uncle Ned" was composed probably in Pittsburgh in 1847 and came into print a year later while Foster was living in Cincinnati. Its publication by W. C. Peters is mentioned above in connection with "Oh! Susanna"; a simultaneous unauthorized edition of the famous song was brought out by W. E. Millet of New York who apparently had received a manuscript copy from William Roark, a resident of Cincinnati and member of the Sable Harmonists minstrel troupe. Though Foster did give a copy of "Uncle Ned" to Roark, it is unlikely that it was "Written & Composed" for him, as the heading states on the first page of music. Roark is pictured on the title page with the five other Sable Harmonists and two black cherubs playing the banjo and tambourine. The music for "Old Uncle Ned" is good early Foster. It has an easy melodic flow, a clever three-part chorus (two tenors and a bass, one might guess), and a little four-measure dance as postlude. But, alas, the heart of the matter here is something that is now dead and embalmed. It is the naïvely grotesque poem itself that certifies the work a genuine museum piece: with all its color and craftsmanship, it is, after all, a curiosity useful mainly for study, like a mummy in a painted case.

"Open Thy Lattice Love" was Stephen Foster's first published song; **"There's a Good Time Coming"** was his second. The first was published in Philadelphia by the firm of G. Willig when Foster was eighteen, the second by [W. C.] Peters & Field of Cincinnati two years later. Both use poems that Foster found in newspapers: "Open Thy Lattice Love," by George P. Morris, was from the *New Mirror*, a New York weekly, and "Good Time Coming," by Charles Mackay, from the *London Daily News*. (If nothing else, this proves that the Foster family home in the Pittsburgh of the 1840's was well supplied with high-class out-of-town newspapers.) "Open Thy Lattice" is a love song, all youthful ardor and romantic images; the musical setting is discreet and pleasant—all in all, a natural for the American parlor trade of 1844. But what a blow it must have been to young Stephen to find his name misprinted on his first published song (L. C. Foster!). "Good Time Coming," with the composer's name now correct, is a more ambitious piece. It is also more recognizable as a Stephen Foster song. The idealistic English poem must have had a strong appeal for the twenty-year-old composer; he gave it a delightful setting full of spirit and conviction.

"Ring de Banjo" appeared in 1851 a few months prior to "Old Folks at Home." It is a splendid minstrel piece that tells of life on another of Foster's mythical plantations. But despite its conventional minstrel-show clichés about the happy lives of the slaves ("De darkey hab no troubles While he's got dis song to sing"), the piece has distinct subversive elements. Verses three through five relate a curious story: a slave is freed and journeys to Kentucky but apparently runs out of money and returns to the plantation ("I turn to massa's door, I lub him all de harder"); subsequently "massa" dies unexpectedly during a banjo recital ("He'll nebber wake again. Ring, ring de banjo!") and the slave runs away, promising to return someday for his lover ("I'll come again my honey, If I hab to work my way"). The story serves as a gentle suggestion—and it is perhaps unique in Foster's works—that life was not all roses and sunshine 'way down south. "Ring de Banjo" is also distinguished by a brief guest appearance of the celebrated Susanna, who is cast as the slave's lover.

"Some Folks": *see* "Hard Times Come Again No More"

"The Song of All Songs" (1863) is what would have been labeled a "novelty song" by Tin Pan Alley music publishers in the twentieth century. Foster compiled all of the verses except the first by stringing together titles and phrases from dozens of popular songs of the day. The trick is not entirely successful. The song has amusing moments, however, and is something of a historical curiosity.

"That's What's the Matter": *see* "Nothing But a Plain Old Soldier"

"There Are Plenty of Fish in the Sea": *see* "If You've Only Got a Moustache"

"There's a Good Time Coming": *see* "Open Thy Lattice Love"

"Thou Art the Queen of My Song" (1859) is a love song, and it contains perhaps more romantic passion than any other Foster song. It is a gentle passion, to be sure, but it is unmistakably present. It is, however, a passion in retrospect: the queen (of the title) has died offstage long before the story begins, joining the sizable "bright and luring throng" of Foster's other heavenly ladies. The song is particularly effective as a tenor solo. The eight-measure postlude should be handled *con espressione*, for it is one of the loveliest instrumental fragments to be found in Foster's works.

"(The) Village Maiden": *see* "Hard Times Come Again No More"

"The Voices That Are Gone" was published posthumously in 1865. It is a slow, waltzing meditation on death. The tune is attractive and expansive, though as a text setting it has moments of awkwardness, such as the accented weak syllable in the word "voices" at the end of the first verse. The title page credits one John P. Cooke as composer of the "Symphonies and Accompaniments." The former consist of an eight-measure prelude and an eight-measure postlude; the latter are smoothly done, though the touches of chromaticism seem somewhat foreign to the composer's style.

"Way Down in Ca-i-ro": *see* "Ah! May the Red Rose Live Alway!"

"We Are Coming, Father Abraam, 300,000 More": *see* "Better Times Are Coming"

"When This Dreadful War Is Ended": *see* "If You've Only Got a Moustache"

"Willie Has Gone to the War": *see* "If You've Only Got a Moustache"

The duet **"Wilt Thou Be Gone, Love?,"** published in 1851, is based on the following passage from the opening of Act III, Scene V, of Shakespeare's *Romeo and Juliet:*

> JULIET: Wilt thou be gone? It is not yet near day.
> It was the nightingale, and not the lark,
> That pierc'd the fearful hollow of thine ear.
> Nightly she sings on yond pomegranate tree.
> Believe me, love, it was the nightingale.
> ROMEO:It was the lark, the herald of the morn;
> No nightingale. Look, love, what envious streaks
> Do lace the severing clouds in yonder East.

Foster's lovely melody and simple harmonies suggest nothing of the "straining harsh discords and unpleasing sharps" that Juliet subsequently attributes to the dreaded lark bringing the morning and the departure of her Romeo.